The UNFORGIVEN

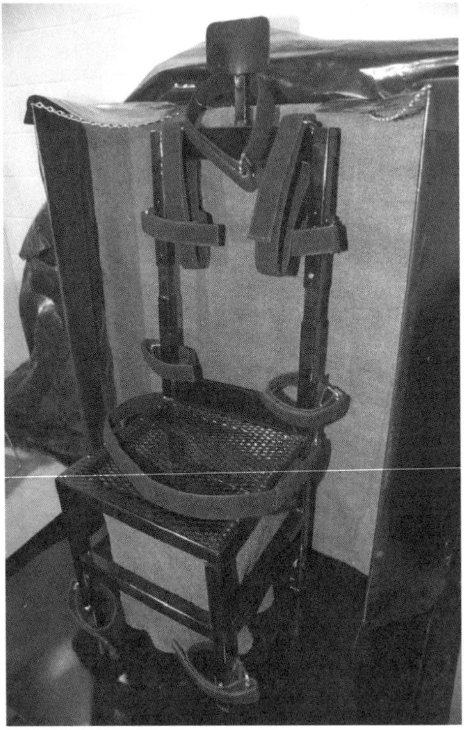

The UNFORGIVEN

Utah's Executed Men

L. KAY GILLESPIE

SIGNATURE BOOKS · SALT LAKE CITY

To
Sheriff John Gillespie
of Tooele, 1830-1915,

and the
Utah State Department
of Corrections

Published 1991. Second edition 1997.

∞ Printed on acid-free paper. Composed, printed, and bound in the United States of America.

LIBRARY OF CONGRESS CATALOGING-IN-PUBLICATION DATA
Gillespie, L. Kay.
The unforgiven : Utah's executed men / by L. Kay Gillespie.—2nd ed.
p. cm.
Includes bibliographical references.
ISBN 1-56085-098-1
1. Capital punishment—Utah—History. 2. Executions and executioners—Utah—History. I. Title.
HV8699.U5G55 1997
364.66'092'2792—dc20
[b] 97-30677
CIP

CONTENTS

ACKNOWLEDGEMENTS

I did not set out to write a book about executed men. My files gradually began to bulge as bits and pieces of the stories of these men began to accumulate. It was, however, the Utah Westerners and the Utah Endowment for the Humanities that provided the incentive, and I am especially grateful to Jerry Dunton, Harold Schindler, John S. McCormick, Delmont Oswald, and Cynthia Buckingham.

I first began talking about a study of executions with Bill Vickrey, director of the Utah State Division of Corrections, and Ken Shulsen, warden at the Utah State Prison. Both were encouraging and helped arrange access to death row and other information. Later through Gary DeLand, director of the Utah State Department of Corrections; Lynn Lund, inspector general with the department; and Dave Franchina, superintendent of institutions, I was able to continue my research, to sit with the execution committee, and to study the execution process. I am grateful to them and to Jerry Cook, warden of the prison; Tom House director of maximum security; and their staffs for their time and patience.

Of course none of this could have been done without Barbara Lopez, my research assistant, who spent countless hours searching, reading, and copying thousands of pages of newsprint.

In addition, I was also able to access prison records and files through the Utah State Archives and would like to thank Terry Ellis and Val Wilson.

Finally I would like to thank Hal Egbert and Richard Holmes for their assistance in reading early versions of the manuscript; Ramona Sessions who entered it all on the computer and who helped me shift, delete, and retrieve it; Weber State University for providing assistance, time, and resources; and my family for their understanding and support.

Whenever any attempt is made to document historical events and to provide the social context of such events, there is the possibility of misinterpretation. I accept full responsibility for such problems. I have attempted to stay within the bounds of what can actually be documented and to limit conjecture—or at least identify it as such when used. This study, building on the work of others, will no doubt be extended and improved upon by future discussions. I hope this book will bring us as a society one step closer toward understanding the terrible truth of capital punishment.

PREFACE TO THE UPDATED EDITION

Two more executions have taken place in Utah since the first edition of *The Unforgiven* appeared in 1991. William Andrews, the last of the "Hi-Fi killers," died by lethal injection on 30 July 1992, and John Albert Taylor died by firing squad on 26 January 1996. I was present at both executions and have used that experience in updating this second edition.

Since 1991 I have also been contacted by readers with additional information regarding the history and events surrounding Utah's executed men. These include:

- a letter from the Lund family with a hand-drawn map showing the location of J. J. Morris's bones;

- a visit from Gary Gilmore's younger brother, Mikal, while he was writing his book about the Gilmore family, *Shot in the Heart* (New York: Doubleday, 1994);

- a brief visit with the babysitter who placed the ad that lead to Shirley Gretzinger's death at the hands of

Ray Dempsey Gardner and who, she told me, never babysat again;

- letters from the families of Enoch Davis and Frank Rose trying to learn more about their ancestors;

- a letter from the family that took in Enoch Davis's two sons and raised them;

- a conversation with former Utah governor J. Bracken Lee regarding the Braasch and Sullivan execution; and

- a conversation with the grandson of Officer Thomas Stagg, whose wife (his grandmother) told him she always believed the other officers shot Stagg, not Patrick Coughlin.

I have attempted to update and revise the text where new information has become available. I hope this knowledge will continue to surface. I remain committed to the continued study of Utah's executions and the execution process. Many things have changed since the first edition was published. Some people are gone, their memories and experiences with them. Some sites no longer exist, while important documents and records have disappeared. Many questions are still unanswered and inconsistencies unresolved.

It is not possible to predict the future of capital punishment in Utah, but it seems safe to say that Utah will continue to execute at about the same rate as it does today. I do not look for much change in the execution of juveniles or adult women, and there undoubtedly will continue to be those who call for the shedding of blood to atone for the sin of murder, in spite of what is presented in this book.

PROLOGUE

It was a sob. Quiet at first, then louder. The silence of the small room became uncomfortable as this sound broke through my shell of "objectivity" and brought me to the realization of where I was: present at an execution. The man lying before me was being put to death.

No one else sobbed—or even shed a tear—as far as I knew. I had attended the meetings as the "execution committee" planned every detail of the lethal injection execution of Arthur Gary Bishop. I had interviewed Bishop shortly after his arrival on death row at the Utah state prison and throughout the next four years. I was with him during much of his time on the "death watch"—the last twenty-four hours prior to his execution. I had entered with the "tie-down team" as he was strapped to the gurney awaiting the lethal injection. His quiet resolve of the previous few weeks was then betrayed on that gurney by the uncontrollable shaking of his knees and thighs.

Now at thirty minutes past midnight on 10 June 1988, three of us stood less than three feet from the gurney waiting for the curtain to be opened. We were his witnesses. The condemned inmate is allowed to "invite" up to five witnesses, but there were only three of us—each there for a different reason. There were others present as well: nine media representatives in a separate room next to ours and government or official witnesses in another area across the execution chamber. As the curtains opened, we could see Art Bishop. He had been convicted and sentenced to die as a child molester and torture-killer of five young boys. He lay on a gurney that looked like a cross. His feet were towards us and the rest of his body to the left at a forty-five degree angle. He was calm, not sedated, as he awaited death; his legs had stopped shaking.

There was no last meal; he chose to fast. Nor were there any last words. His final statement was prepared a few days before. With care and precision he wrote a page and a half of what he wanted to say. During my last visit with him in his maximum security cell, he asked me to read it to see if it "sounded all right." With minor changes, this was the statement that was handed to the press after he was pronounced dead:

> As I prepare to die, there are a few last words I wish to leave with you. With great sadness and remorse I realize that I allowed myself to be misled by Satan, and as a result my life has been marked by wicked, perverse and depraved actions. Now the mistakes of my life are being rehashed by the news media, sometimes with sensationalism and exaggerations. There are two especially pernicious rumors I wish to squelch right now. First, I have been convicted and sentenced for all murders for which I'm responsible—there are no others. And Second, I have never been sexually abused by anyone.
>
> At this time I want to offer again my most profound and heartfelt apologies to my victims'

families. I am truly sorry. I have tried my best to empathize with their grief and devastation, and I hope they come to know of my concerns and prayers for them.

I wish to offer a word of thanks to the fine people who, by their selfless acts, have provided so much comfort and succor to my family at this difficult time. I also thank the numerous people who have sent me letters of encouragement and concern; your kindness and thoughtfulness have touched my heart. I have been unable to respond to all of your letters, but I will never forget them.

By accepting my execution I do not consider myself a courageous hero or a noble martyr, or that I'm "giving up," or that I'm "going out in a blaze of glory," as some people have suggested. I am merely accepting my just punishment as my conscience dictates I must. I do have hope that my death may help others to find relief and forgiveness; even if it doesn't, it is still a necessary requirement because of my past heinous crimes. Though perhaps too little too late, I am doing the right thing now.

I leave this life with no ill feelings towards anyone, and I pray that the peace of God may rest upon each and every one of you. I know of God's love, patience and compassion, and have found comfort in that knowledge. When I kneel before Christ in the next life, having a perfect recollection of all my guilt, with a broken heart I will humbly plead: "Jesus, thou Son of God, have mercy on my soul."

There were no "throes of death," no twitching or last gasps. In our small cubicle there was no talking. In the next room, where the media representatives were gathered, I could hear them as they watched the gurney with one eye, the clock with the other. "He's stopped breathing." "What time is it?" "It's 00:14 a.m." "He's dead."

The white-faced clock on the wall measured time by twenty-four-hour military standards. It was 00:14 a.m. as the medical examiner entered the execution chamber. Official time of death: 00:16 a.m.

I am often asked how I felt watching someone be put to death—as though I could distill my feelings, conflicting and contradictory as they were, into a simple statement. And yet that was one of the reasons I chose to be involved in the execution process, not only to understand and explore my own feelings but to share with others what the process is like and how it affects those involved.

I felt nothing. As I review my notes they are objective and removed. I was an observer, there to document the process. But as I reflect on that night and on the night of Pierre Dale Selby's execution (Utah's first by lethal injection), in which I also participated, I am only now beginning to allow myself to feel. I remember my palms getting sweaty as I tried to hold my pen and take notes of Bishop's final minutes. I am told by family and friends that I seemed withdrawn after each execution and that I was short-tempered and less patient with my children. I also remember a tensing throughout my whole body, and some indigestion. I was not conscious of this until a few days after each execution when I felt a gradual relaxing. Only then did I realize how tense I had been.

I know that others involved in the execution process experience similar feelings. Some require psychological counseling afterward. Others experience depression and uncontrollable crying spells. Some are still employed at the prison; others are not. This does not surprise me. During the hours I spent on the "death watch," when the condemned is isolated from the rest of the prison and under constant visual supervision just steps from the room in which he will die, several of the men selected for this watch made a point of talking to me to express their feelings about their part in the process. One man told me he had always favored the death penalty, but now watching the condemned man prepare to die and being an actual participant in that death, he wondered if "we" as a society were doing the right thing. Another told me how his attitude had changed. He had guarded the condemned on a daily basis in his maximum security death-row cell. Now as a participant on the death watch he felt uncomfortable. "It would be different if he were a 'crud' but he is a nice, gentle person. I'm not sure we are doing the right thing." Another explained how he used to be "gung-ho" for capital punishment, but since this experience he wasn't so sure anymore.

I have read statements by the public and seen news articles reporting the great number of "average" citizens who volunteer to conduct executions—particularly after highly publicized or heinous crimes. "Pulling the plug," "pulling the trigger," "arranging the noose," "releasing the pellets," "inserting the needles"—all sound so simple and are so easily said with reference to people we do not know and who are portrayed as cold-blooded monsters. If it were only so, it would be easy. What happens, however, is that our own humanity becomes meshed with that of the condemned. In those last moments we see another human being, who is perhaps too human, being prepared to die. I say this with full awareness of the victim and the victim's family. There is no excuse for this kind of crime. I intend no defense of the capital offender, only to suggest that in any person's death we all share our own helplessness and uncertainty. Perhaps today we should follow the old "Halifax Gibbet Law" which required as a condemned person was brought forth for public execution that "every man there doth either take hold of the rope or putteth forth his arm so near to the same as he can get, in token that he is willing to see justice executed" (in Frank A. King, "Thirteenpence—Halfpenny for the Hangman," *Justice of the Peace and Local Government Review* [5 April 1958]: 216).

Of course Pierre Dale Selby deserved to die for the torture-killing of three innocent people. Of course Arthur Gary Bishop deserved to die, as he himself believed, for the brutal deaths of five innocent boys. But to execute with pleasure and to celebrate it from a distance is far different from being an actual participant in the process of taking life.

There are various reactions among those who participate. Some are, on the outside, professional, aloof, removed. Some seem to derive a certain satisfaction from their involvement. As Selby was being led from his cell to the execution chamber, two men at one of the doors were talking. One said, loud enough for Selby to hear, "This is the payoff that makes it all worth it." He was quickly quieted by a supervisor as we passed by.

I did not participate in the execution of Gary Gilmore, although I was present when John Albert Taylor died by the same method. It seems to me that the innovation of execution by lethal injection has brought a new distance to the execution process. Earlier executions in Utah and other states were not such sterile events. The warden was often invited to share the condemned man's last meal. The condemned's last words expresssed gratitude to the guards and other prison personnel, and his last hours were often spent in conversation with his keepers. Some of this is still present and the degree differs perhaps from state to state, but for the most part, the process has become clinical, distant, sterile, medicalized. Even the terminology–gurney, solution, I.V.–sounds more like an operation than an execution, more like a surgical procedure than a sentence of the justice system. There is no humane way to execute, but we pretend there is. In the words of one minister after he witnessed an execution by lethal injection: "I'm angry and I'm just every bit as angry about the way it was done. Just very clinical. I would almost rather have seen some pain to indicate that we wanted to see death as it really is" (Father Ron Cloutier, on the Phil Donahue television talk show, Dec. 1983).

As a general rule the condemned is first put into a chemically-induced sleep and then the lethal drugs enter his body—to stop respiration, to stop brain function, and to stop the heart. In some states other drugs are also included. Early lethal-injection executions caused the legs of the condemned to jerk spasmodically. This was distressing to the witnesses, so a substance was included that would eliminate this. More recently, after the condemned was put to sleep, he sometimes snored. Again this offended the witnesses and so more substances were included. It is as though we have tried to totally camouflage the procedure to avoid any semblance of death. The fact may be that in many subtle ways, lethal injection is more cruel than previous methods.

The process of execution is long and tedious. Thousands of trivial details must be arranged and planned for. As I attended the Utah planning committee's meetings, I was constantly amazed at all the contingencies that arose. No dramatic production was ever staged with more care and deliberation. The actors, the stage, the rehearsals, the publicity—even the potential *deus ex machina*—all part of this "gala." (The word gala, by the way, comes from "gallows," the celebration and events that took place as a part of public hangings.) I do not mean to imply by any of this that the process is artificial. My notes from these meetings indicate sincerity and concern for the condemned as well as for his and his victims' families.

For those who wonder, "How much planning does it take to arrange five rifles or to insert a needle?" consider the following, while bearing in mind that the object is to conduct an execution that will be as efficient as possible and that will be under constant public scrutiny and criticism at every step:

Who will be allowed to attend and how will they be selected?

When is the best time to conduct an execution and how will the time affect protestors, supporters, and the other prison inmates?

Who will actually inject the lethal dose and how will this person(s) be selected, brought to the execution site, paid, and protected?

How will the prescription be obtained for drugs to kill when the medical profession refuses to participate in the process?

How can the inmate be secured in such a way as to insure humane and caring treatment while at the same time preventing him from taking his own life or injuring those around him?

At what point in the process is it too late to turn back? When can a stay of execution no longer stay the process and who is to make that decision?

How can a circus atmosphere be avoided in order to separate the wheels of justice from personal vendettas and public revenge?

There are many other issues. These merely give a sense of the complexity that needs to be addressed. The overall policies and procedures resulted in a technical manual of over 600 pages.

Why bother with all of this? Why have I researched and written these stories? I am not opposed to capital punishment. I believe a democratic society has the right to inflict such punishment. I have some reservations about what I see as the capriciousness of our present justice system and the inherent biases of law enforcement and zealous prosecutors. Yet my intention is not to right any wrongs—only to assure that those lives taken through the penalty of death are remembered. After all, the purpose of any social sanction is to assure future compliance with and respect for law. This cannot be accomplished if those who are the objects of societal punishment are forgotten and their crimes and deaths never reviewed.

Perhaps through the stories of Utah's executed men, each of us will have the chance as did those in Halifax to vicariously put our hands on the rope and announce our willingness to be a part of justice dispensed. And if it occasionally feels uncomfortable, we can then review our own commitment and responsibility to see that society does not carelessly toy with those lives it chooses to forfeit.

1.

BLOOD ATONEMENT

On 21 January 1878 the case of Wallace Wilkerson versus Utah was heard by the Supreme Court of the United States. Wilkerson, convicted of killing William Baxter in a saloon argument over cards on 11 June 1877, had been sentenced to die by firing squad. His appeal was the first eighth amendment challenge to the death penalty ever heard by the Supreme Court. The court ruled "that execution by shooting was not prohibited by the Eighth Amendment's cruel and unusual punishment clause, in that the method used (quite apart from the act of dying) did not entail torture or unnecessary cruelty."[1]

This challenge points to the commonly held belief in the uniqueness of Utah's death penalty. Utah allows the condemned to choose between a firing squad and another form of death, originally beheading or hanging but now lethal injection. However, several states in addition to Utah offer more than one form of execution. Only Utah still provides the option of a firing squad, but other states (as well as the military) have used firing squads. Those states in which more than one method of execution is provided generally allow the condemned to choose how he or she will die.

Utah is unique in that the state's practice of allowing the condemned his choice of execution stems from a religious belief: only through choosing a method of execution which results in blood being "spilled" (or shed) can the condemned hope to receive forgiveness in the next life. The existence and evolution of this belief—known in Mormon theology as "blood atonement"—is complex.

After arriving in the Salt Lake valley in July 1847, early Mormon settlers established the state of Deseret, ruled by the laws of God's new kingdom. The area they settled belonged to Mexico, but this did not daunt their zeal. Under the leadership of Brigham Young, they planned for settlements encompassing parts of the present states of Utah, Idaho, Arizona, Nevada, California, Colorado, New Mexico, Wyoming, and Oregon. The area passed to the United States in 1848, and territorial status was granted in 1850. The first territorial legislature enacted a criminal code based on one originally created by the general assembly of the state of Deseret, a body controlled by Mormon leaders.[2] The punishment prescribed for first-degree murder was execution with the condemned allowed to choose among firing squad, hanging, or beheading.

Mormon leaders believed that Jesus' blood did not forgive murderers, who could personally "atone" for their sin only by offering their own blood. Brigham Young, for example, maintained: "There are sins that men commit for which they cannot receive forgiveness in this world, or in that which is to come, and if they had their eyes open to see their true condition, they would be perfectly willing to have their blood spilt upon the ground, that the smoke thereof might ascend to heaven as an offering for their sins; and the smoking incense would atone for their sin; whereas, if such is not the case, they will stick to them and remain upon them in the spirit world."[3] Young's counselor Jedediah M. Grant agreed: "I say, that there are men and women that I would advise to go to the President immediately, and ask him to appoint a committee to attend to their case; and then let a place be selected, and let that committee shed their blood."[4] On another occasion he argued, "Brethren and sisters, we want you to repent and forsake your sins. And you who have committed sins that cannot be forgiven through baptism, let your blood be shed . . . before God as an atonement for your sins . . ."[5] Apostle Heber C. Kimball also echoed these sentiments: "I think it would be an excellent thing for this people to be sanctified from such persons, and have them cleansed from our midst, by making an atonement."[6] On another occasion he commented, "If a man has shed innocent blood, he will have to pay the atonement, or he never can atone for his sin."[7]

In 1888 beheading was dropped as an alternative. No one had ever selected it, even after an appeal for the use of the guillotine appeared in the *Daily Ogden Junction* on 17 May 1879 following a particularly "messy" execution—ironically, that of Wallace Wilkerson:

> The execution of Wallace Wilkerson at Provo yesterday affords another illustration of the brutal exhibitions of inquisitorial torture that have of late disgraced . . . the country and which have in some States so shocked the natural sensibilities of the people that extreme punishment has been abrogated from pure disgust excited by the sickening spectacles of rotten ropes, ignorantly or carelessly adjusted nooses or inexperienced marksmen. These disgusting scenes are invariably ascribed to accidental causes, but they have become so horrifyingly frequent that some other method of judicial murder should be adopted. The French guillotine never fails. The swift falling knife flashes in the light, a dull thud

is heard and all is over. It is eminently more merciful to the victim than our bungling atrocities, and the ends of justice are as fully secured.

Tolerance for capital punishment has remained steady in Utah, with many Mormons basing their support on the religious beliefs of their nineteenth-century leaders. In a letter dated 20 September 1978 and addressed to Mormon church president Spencer W. Kimball, Thomas B. McAffee, then editor of the *Utah Law Review,* asked several questions about the church's view on the death penalty and blood atonement. Responding on official letterhead at the request of the First Presidency, Apostle Bruce R. McConkie wrote: "We do *not* believe that it is necessary for men in this day to shed their own blood to receive a remission of sins. This is said with a full awareness of what I and others have written and said on this subject in times past." He went on to say that the law of blood atonement "has *not* been given to the church at anytime in this dispensation. It has *no application* whatever to anyone now living whether a member or a nonmember of the Church. . . . There simply is no such thing among us as a doctrine of blood atonement that grants a remission of sins or confers any other benefit upon a person because his own blood is shed for sins."

In response to McAffee's question whether statements of past Mormon leaders on blood atonement represented the official position of the church, McConkie wrote, "The answer, as indicated in the comments above set forth, is that they do *not.* The statements pertain to *a theoretical principle* that has been *neither revealed to nor practiced by us.*" McConkie concluded his letter by addressing McAffee's final question if the church's belief in blood atonement made any difference in how the death penalty is carried out: "As far as I can see there is no difference between a firing squad, an electric chair, a gas chamber, or hanging. Death is death and I would interpret the shedding of man's blood in legal executions as a figurative expression which means the taking of life. There seems to me to be no present significance as to whether an execution is by a firing squad or in some other way. I, of course, deleted my article on 'hanging' from the Second Edition of *Mormon Doctrine* because of the reasons here mentioned."

McConkie affirmed the position of the Mormon church in favor of capital punishment: "We believe in capital punishment. In a revelation to Joseph Smith, on February 9, 1831, the Lord said: 'And now, behold, I speak unto the church. Thou shalt not kill; and he that kills shall not have forgiveness in this world, nor in the world to come. And again, I say, thou shalt not kill; but he that killeth shall die' (D&C 42:18-19)."[8]

When Utah's largely Mormon legislature changed the state's capital punishment statute in 1980, it replaced death by hanging with death by lethal injection but retained death by firing squad. Old perceptions do not change quickly. In 1984 Arthur Gary Bishop, eagle scout and former Mormon missionary, was sentenced to die for killing five young boys. Given the option of dying by lethal injection or firing squad, Bishop appealed for guidance to the First Presidency. Through Clyde Archer, his lay bishop, he received a response from Gordon B. Hinckley, counselor to President Spencer W. Kimball. At the insistence of Hinckley the letter was not shown to Bishop (or to anyone else) but was read to him by Archer, accompanied by Heber Guertz. Archer retained the original letter. On 11 June 1987 while awaiting execution, Bishop told me that Hinckley indicated the method of execution did not matter. Bishop implied that according to Hinckley, blood atonement ended with the crucifixion of Jesus Christ and the manner of execution today has no effect.[9]

A more recent statement about the Latter-day Saint church and capital punishment appeared in the *Intermountain Catholic* on 17 July 1987. The occasion was the execution of Pierre Dale Selby, Utah's first by lethal injection, and the speaker was Jerry Cahill of the church's public communication office: "I guess what we are saying is that if the state and federal laws provide for capital punishment, we are bound by those laws. The U.S. allows for capital punishment, so we would go along with the decision here. In Great Britain, there is no capital punishment, so we would be against it there." If Cahill was speaking in his capacity as spokesperson for the LDS church, he implies, contrary to what McConkie said, the LDS church's position on capital punishment depends on the laws of the land.

NOTES

1. *Criminal Justice Abstracts,* 13 (2): 292, June 1981, Sarah T. Dike, Part I. Also Wilkerson v. Utah, 99 U.S. 130 (1878).

2. Martin R. Gardner, "Illicit Legislative Motivation as a Sufficient Condition for Unconstitutionality Under the Establishment Clause—A Case for Consideration: The Utah Firing Squad," *Washington University Law Quarterly* (1979): 450-51.

3. *Journal of Discourses,* 26 vols. (Liverpool: Latter-day Saints' Book Depot, 1855-86), 4:53.

4. Ibid., 49.

5. Ibid., 5.

6. Ibid., 7:17.

7. Ibid., 236.

8. Bruce R. McConkie to Thomas B. McAffee, 18 Oct. 1978, copy in my possession.

9. I have not seen this letter and rely on what I was told by Art Bishop and in conversation with Heber Guertz on 19 June 1991.

2.

MOUNTAIN JUSTICE

In the American west executions did not always proceed according to protocol. Vigilante justice was a popular concept (though the number of documented incidents is small). The earliest record of an "execution"—that of a native American named Patsowits in southern Utah—was probably an instance of this "mountain justice."

John W. Gunnison, a government surveyor who came to Utah with the Stansbury expedition, recorded the following on 29 April 1850: "Patsowits, one of the Utah Indians has been discovered lurking about here [shores of Great Salt Lake]. He is accused of killing an emigrant near Sampete [sic] last week & has been driven from Utah. 5 p.m.—A company is pointed out near Mill Creek who are to shoot & bury him. He strove manfully against being bound in the council house—but no earthly mercy is shown."[1]

Historian Dale Morgan described this incident in detail:

> The execution of Patsowits constitutes almost a lost episode in Utah History. It was said to have been

he who killed Joseph Higbee in the Fort Utah fight. He escaped after that battle and occupied himself killing stock. On April 21 Isaac Morley in Sanpete Valley wrote Brigham Young he had learned from the Utes that Patsowits had killed six cattle, two mules, and two horses in Salt Lake Valley and was threatening to kill the cattle of the Mormons and of the Ute chief, Walker, in Sanpete Valley. On April 8 Isaac Higbee wrote from Fort Utah that he understood Patsowits to be at Great Salt Lake. "He and his brother have been killing cattle since the war with the Indians and threatened to kill every white man that he can. We have been searching for him to kill him, but have not found him yet. But we found his brother and have killed him. We wish you would search for him, and, if he can be found in your valley, to kill him before he can do any more mischief." On the following day, April 29, a letter arrived from Sanpete Valley reporting that "Baker who went to Sanpete with the provisions recently sent to the settlers there, imprudently started on his return trip alone. On the way he was met by two Ute Indians to whom he gave some powder, after which they shot him with his own powder." Patsowits accordingly was taken into custody and the [LDS church] Historians's Office Journal for April 29 records he was tried and sentenced to die: "The Indian was very boisterous, talking long and loud. He was finally put into the hands of three or four men for safe keeping. He fought desperately, when they attempted to bind him, and it took five men to hold him while he was being pinioned. He finally became more quiet and was taken in Levi Savage's wagon outside the city, where chapl[a]in [John] Kay and the Sheriff [James Ferguson] administered his last religious rites before he died. Several persons were present and witnessed

> the execution." Seemingly, the Indian was not shot, as Gunnison's journal entry would imply, but garrotted; from his book Gunnison writes (147) that Patsowits was "caught and killed by the bowstring." Apparently this was the first formal execution in Utah history.[2]

Hosea Stout, an early Mormon, also wrote about this death in his journal for Monday, 29 April 1850: "Pat Souette [Patsowits?] was arrested & tried & nepoed [opened] today. He escaped over the mountains with some others in the Utah war & came back & was trying to way lay & kill all the whites he could catch alone. One man had been killed coming from San Pete here lately." The editor of Stout's journals, Juanita Brooks, explained what "nepoed" probably meant: "Since it is 'open' spelled backwards, there is a conjecture that it might refer to a practice of disemboweling a murdered man, filling the abdominal cavity with rocks, and throwing the body into a stream or lake." Brooks also notes that "the young Indian who was 'nepoed' on April 27 [29], 1850, did not have a public trial but was condemned by a military group."[3]

These accounts leave a number of issues ambiguous. They suggest that Patsowit's brother had also been killed by the settlers or military authorities. Perhaps then the brother's was the first "execution." There are also questions about how official or legal the "execution" was and by what method Patsowits died—whether shot, "garrotted", or "nepoed."

Another early execution apparently occurred on a wagon trail. The company was traveling toward California and as the group was passing Devil's Gate, one traveler killed another. Devil's Gate is located near Independence Rock in Wyoming. The company held a trial with a jury and condemned the man to death. After he was attended by a clergyman, he was hung from the end of a wagon pole

Patrick Coughlin awaiting execution by firing squad at Sage Hollow near Woodruff, Utah, 15 December 1896. Courtesy Charlie Trentleman and the *Ogden Standard-Examiner.*

because there were no trees in the vicinity.[4] The wagon master would have had legal authority to order the execution, as does a ship's captain.

William (Wild Bill) Hickman in his "autobiography" recounts a similar hanging which occurred while he was guiding a wagon train from Utah to California. A man named Hensley killed John Watson, another member of the party. Hensley apparently took offense at something Watson had said and later that night shot him in the head while he slept. A trial was held with a jury composed of members of Hickman's train and another train they met coming from California. Hensley was found guilty and hanged on the spot.[5] There are many who question Hickman's authority to implement such action.

References to two other executions have been found. In 1896 the *Salt Lake Tribune* refers to an Indian condemned for "ravishing and murdering a white woman" and executed at the "white bridge" over the Jordan River. Also, the *Deseret News* refers to the execution of a man in 1862: "A man whose name is not available was shot in the county jail yard in Tooele for murder." Neither the name of this man nor the exact date or details of his crime have been documented. The only Tooele execution so far identified occurred in 1866 and took place on the bench above Tooele.

Excluding the above accounts, I have documented forty-nine legal executions in Utah since 1847. Two double-executions with both men dying simultaneously have ocurred; in three other double-executions both men were executed but at different times.

Of Utah's forty-nine executions, forty were by firing squad, six by hanging, and three by lethal injection. Each of these three methods of execution was carefully prescribed by tradition and statute.

The firing squad usually consisted of five men, generally volunteers from the sheriff's office in the county where the crime occurred. Members of the firing squad are concealed

Drawing of the hanging apparatus used to execute Charles Thiede, 8 August 1896.

in tents, behind curtains, or some other device to protect their identities. Each man has a rifle; one contains a blank cartridge. A target is pinned over the heart of the person to be executed. The command to fire is given and each of the men shoots at the target. Usually the firing squad is placed no more than fifty feet from the condemned, although the distance in Utah has varied from twenty-three to one hundred and eighty feet.

As a general rule the condemned to be hanged climbed a gallows. Once on the platform, he stood over a trap door through which he dropped once the noose had been placed around his neck. The last hanging in Utah occurred in 1956.

In 1896 a unique form of hanging was attempted. Charles Thiede, condemned to die for killing his wife, stood on the ground with a rope around his neck. The rope went up through a pulley system and along an upright beam with a large weight attached at the other end. Three men held and released ropes, only one of which was attached to the weight. The condemned was supposed to be yanked from the ground and his neck broken when the weight was released. The device was only used once. Thiede was yanked off the ground, but his neck was not broken and he was strangled to death.

Three of the last four executions in Utah have been by lethal injection. Pierre Dale Selby was executed on 28 August 1987, Arthur Gary Bishop on 10 June 1988, and William Andrews, 30 July 1992. In each case the condemned was brought into a small room and strapped to a gurney about three and a half to four feet above the floor. Eight straps were tightened around his body (two at the ankles, one at the knees, thighs, waist, and chest, and one around each wrist). An I.V. was started in each arm, one as a backup should the other become clogged. When the witnesses were assembled, the curtain to the execution chamber was opened and the warden gave a signal to two executioners who waited behind a one-way glass mirror. At this point, the lethal solution

Gurney used in the lethal injection of Pierre Dale Selby. Photographed after the execution, 28 August 1987. Courtesy Clyde Mueller and the *Ogden Standard-Examiner.*

was introduced into the bloodstream. Death followed anywhere from three to four minutes later.

Of the forty-nine men formally executed in Utah, forty-two were white, two hispanic, three black, and two Native American. In the past, challenges have been made on the basis of race and ethnicity. In a 1987 appeal to the U.S. Supreme Court, attorneys for condemned inmate Richard McClesky argued the death penalty was racially discriminatory in that those whose victims were white, especially if the offender was black, were more likely to receive the death penalty than those whose victims were black. Opponents of the death penalty have also argued that more blacks than whites are executed. In making their ruling in the McClesky case, the Supreme Court stated: "Apparent disparities in sentencing are an inevitable part of our criminal justice system. . . . Where the discretion that is fundamental to our criminal process is involved, we decline to assume that what is unexplained is invidious."[6]

The racial distribution of executions does not appear to be disproportional to the general racial distribution in Utah. Data about the racial distribution of victims are more ambiguous, although race does not appear to have been a major factor in Utah executions. Of the fifty-nine victims (excluding the Mountain Meadows massacre), fifty-eight were white and one was black. There have been no executions where the victims were hispanic or Native American.

The extent to which religion has been a factor is more difficult to ascertain. Early relations in Utah were polarized along Mormon/non-Mormon lines. Animosity and suspicion existed between both groups. Gentile newspapers asserted that Mormon criminals were not pursued with the same vigor accorded non-Mormon offenders. A 3 November 1889 editorial in the *Valley Tan* charged:

> The execution of Ferguson we have been informed, is the first that has ever taken place in this

> Territory by a regular judicial sentence. Of the many murders that have taken place here, the perpetrators of them have in all instances escaped, or no notice whatever has been taken of their crime, the general belief being, that they were authorized or commanded by those who wield a despotic power over the lives and actions of the deluded and fanatical people that dwell in this Territory. . . . We . . . cannot help thinking that [Ferguson's] fate could have been different if he had been a professed Mormon.

Of the forty-nine men executed in Utah, twenty-seven were non-Mormon, eight Mormon, and fourteen unknown. This is not representative of the population in general, but most non-Mormon executed men had recently come to Utah from out-of-state or were passing through at the time of their crimes. This begs the question, but it could indicate the presence of some degree of xenophobia or the reality of Utah's sparse population and geographical location as well as religious discrimination.

Utah has never executed or sentenced a woman to death—although women have committed heinous crimes (see chapter eight). In the United States in general, women have been protected from the death penalty. Although the homicide arrest rate for women has been constant with and almost identical to that of men, only thirty-seven women have been executed in the United States since 1900. The last woman executed was Velma Barfield in 1984, and she was the first since the California execution of "Ma" Duncan in 1962. Only thirteen states have executed women. At the present time, of over three thousand condemned inmates on death row across the United States, only forty-six are women. (See my book on executed women, *Dancehall Ladies: The Crimes and Executions of America's Condemned Women* [Canham, MD: University Press of America, 1997].)

Utah has never executed anyone under the age of

eighteen, although juveniles have committed terrible crimes (see chapter eight). The youngest were Harry Thorne and Chauncy Millard—both eighteen at the time of execution. The oldest were John D. Lee, sixty-four, and Edward McGowan, fifty-one. The age distribution of the executed men in Utah is as follows:

Under 20	3
20-29	18
30-39	16
40-49	5
50 & over	2
Unknown	5

The death penalty has been prescribed for a variety of crimes throughout the United States, including rape, kidnapping, hijacking, skyjacking, and espionage. In Utah, executions have been carried out only for murder or for being an accomplice to murder. Of the forty-four crimes resulting in the state's forty-nine executions, seventeen murders were committed with robbery or financial gain as the motive; thirteen were the result of personal/family disputes or arguments; eleven were committed with a specific intent to kill; and three to satisfy sexual desire. A gun was used in thirty-one homicides; a knife in four; strangling in four; and in five, bludgeoning using an axe, a gun, a flat iron, a hammer, and a small mallet. Conspicuously absent is poisoning.

These crimes were committed in thirteen of Utah's twenty-nine counties. Most of them occurred, as expected, along the more densely populated Wasatch Front:

Salt Lake County	20
Utah County	4
Weber County	5

Summit County	3
Tooele County	2
Carbon County	2
Beaver County	1
Davis County	1
Duchesne County	2
Iron County	1
Rich County	1
San Juan County	1
Washington County	1

The time between crime and execution was varied widely. The execution of William Andrews in 1992 occurred eighteen years after the killing of three people in the Ogden Hi-Fi Shop. Earlier, executions were conducted soon after conviction. In Tooele in 1866, Thomas Sutton was executed eight days after killing a man named White. In 1862 Jason Luce was executed for cutting the throat of a man named Bunton thirty-six days after his crime. William Cockroft killed his neighbor with a shotgun blast over a water dispute. He was executed 21 September 1861, fifty-one days later. Thomas Ferguson was hanged forty-one days after killing his employer.

The time between William Andrews's crime and execution was by no means the longest. The Mountain Meadows massacre occurred in 1857. Twenty years later, 23 March 1877, John D. Lee was brought back to the site of the massacre where he was executed while seated on his coffin.

One other execution—actually a double execution—caused public and official concern about the delay. On 22 October 1949, the opening day of the Utah deer hunt, Melvin Braasch and LeRoy Sullivan killed, execution style, a young service station attendant in Beaver, Utah. Both were sentenced to die but received four different dates of execution before the sentences were actually carried out. Governor J.

Bracken Lee became so frustrated he threatened to charge the U.S. government for the costs of keeping the condemned alive. They were both eventually executed by firing squad while sitting side by side on 11 May 1956, almost seven years after their crime.

Excluding participants in the Mountain Meadows massacre, twenty-one accomplices were involved in the forty-three Utah crimes resulting in execution. Only five accomplices were executed for their roles in the crimes; sixteen were given sentences other than death.

John McCormick (also known as Jack Emerson) was sentenced to life in prison. After five years he was pardoned as the last official act of Governor Eli H. Murray. He was an accomplice to Fred Hopt who was executed on 11 August 1887.

Fred George was sentenced to life in prison rather than death because of his youth at the time of the crime. He was paroled on 20 December 1902 and less than two years later, on 19 June 1904, was granted a full pardon "because of the exemplary life he had led." He was an accomplice to Patrick Coughlin who was executed on 15 December 1896.

John Murray (also known as Mike Connors) was sentenced to life in prison. He was involved in the robbery of the Savings and Thrift Shop but was not with J. J. Morris at the time of the killing. No further records are available. Morris was executed on 30 April 1912.

"Red" was the third accomplice in the grocery store holdup and killing of George Fassell. Harry Thorne was executed on 26 September 1912 and Thomas Riley on 24 October 1912. "Red" was never caught or heard from again.

John Corier and Robert Zaffy were accomplices to Frank Romeo who was executed on 20 February 1913. Corier was granted a separate trial and sentenced to life in prison on the jury's recommendation for mercy. Zaffy was sentenced to die with Romeo, but his sentence was commuted to life in prison by the Board of Pardons the day before his scheduled execution. The board reasoned that Zaffy had been drinking and was not as culpable as Romeo.

"Unknown," a suspected accomplice to Joe Hill who was executed on 19 November 1915, was never arrested or heard from again. The crime for which Hill was executed involved two men. As Hill and his accomplice made their get-a-way, one eyewitness said she heard one of the men say, "Oh, Bob." Others have surmised the accomplice might have been Otto Applequist, who was known to be in the Salt Lake City area with Hill.

Martha, the common-law wife of George H. Gardner who was executed on 31 August 1923, was originally charged with murder. Her first trial ended in a hung jury after twenty-seven hours of deliberation. She was never retried.

Arthur Hayes was tried for murder and given a life sentence on the jury's recommendation for mercy. His sentence was eventually overturned by Utah's supreme court and a new trial was ordered. At his new trial he was found guilty of second degree robbery, given a five-year prison sentence, and paroled on 16 October 1926. He was accomplice to Henry C. Hett (also known as George Allen) who was executed on 20 February 1925.

Joseph Eli Marenger (also known as Ralph Sanders) and Noel E. White (also known as George Williams) were accomplices to Ralph Seyboldt, who was executed on 15 January 1926. Marenger pleaded guilty to second degree murder and was given a twenty-year sentence. He was paroled from the Utah state prison on 1 July 1930 after serving almost seven years. He went to California to live with his mother and sister. White, who was sixteen at the time of the crime, also pleaded guilty to second degree murder and was given a twenty-year sentence. His sentence was commuted by the Board of Pardons after he served a little over ten years. A third accomplice, Leland Elmer, pleaded guilty to attempted robbery.

Roverda Avery, wife of Walter Robert Avery who was executed on 5 February 1943, was originally arrested as an accomplice since she drove him to the robbery and waited in the car outside while the killing took place. She was later released.

LeRoy Edward Ritchie was given a life sentence after the jury recommended leniency. He was never paroled. On 15 May 1954 he died of tuberculosis in an Ogden, Utah, sanitarium where he had been sent for treatment. He was an accomplice to James Joseph Roedl, who was executed on 13 July 1945.

Wilma Tulley was in a police car when a policeman was shot. She then escaped but was later caught in Nevada and provided evidence against Don Jesse Neal. She was released and never prosecuted. It has been suggested she actually fired the shot which killed the officer and that Neal protected her. Neal was executed on 1 July 1955.

Keith Roberts and William Andrews were tried separately—Roberts alone and Andrews with Pierre Dale Selby. Roberts was paroled in May 1987 after serving approximately thirteen years for aggravated robbery. Andrews was executed on 30 July 1992. Selby was executed 28 August 1988.

NOTES

1. See Brigham Madsen, *Exploring the Great Salt Lake: The Stansbury Expedition of 1849-50* (Salt Lake City: University of Utah Press, 1989), 380.

2. Ibid., 380-81n.

3. Juanita Brooks, ed., *On The Mormon Frontier: The Diary of Hosea Stout,* 2 vols. (Salt Lake City: University of Utah Press, Utah State Historical Society), 1:368, 368n38, 527n27.

4. Arthur T. Challis quotes S. S. Goode in "Handbook of Utah First Facts: 1540-1895," M.S. thesis, University of Utah, 1959.

5. Bill Hickman, *Brigham's Destroying Angel: Being the Life Confessions and Startling Disclosures of the Notorious Bill Hickman, The Danite Chief of Utah* (Salt Lake City: Shepard Publishing Company, 1904), 75-80.

6. Justice Powell, writing for the majority opinion, quoted in *Chicago Tribune,* 23 April 1987.

3.

MORMONS AND GENTILES

The early history of crime in Utah is difficult to follow. Often the line between religious transgression and crime was blurred. Both sin and crime were tried in ecclesiastical courts convened by Mormon bishops or other religious leaders. The appointment of territorial judges did not simplify matters. The continual dispute between "outsider" judges and local leaders led to chaos and manipulation of the judiciary. Judges accused Mormons of trampling on the Constitution and destroying the separation of church and state. Mormons called judges "carpetbaggers" and accused them of using their positions to persecute people because of their religious beliefs.

No early data tracking crime or murder rates are available. There is reason to believe that a fairly large number of homicides took place along the Wasatch Front. Some deaths occurred from Indian raids, some from fights and arguments, some from vigilantes, and still others from demands for "blood atonement." Some perpetrators were arrested, others were either never found or never prosecuted. A 26

April 1859 editorial in the non-Mormon *Valley Tan* responding to an editorial in a "Mormon" newspaper focused the problem:

> There have been more murders committed and more blood shed in the county, within the last eight months, than before or since its organization. We clip the above from the Church Organ of the 20th inst. and it is a piece of the whole which abound in self-laudation, and hypocritically assumes what a good people we are. After assuming that innumerable murders have been committed within a specified time, the very period when the "Gentiles" have been more numerous than heretofore, the Editor, although he does not say it, seeks to leave the impression that they are the offending parties. It is a species of deceit and chicanery peculiar to Mormonism, and so long practiced that we are led to believe that they esteem falsehood a virtue when it can be made to suit their own purposes.

According to available records, few executions took place between 1847 and 1878. One of the first documented cases involving a form of Utah justice is that of Jean Baptiste. Baptiste was a grave digger at the Salt Lake City cemetery. In 1862 he was arrested for grave robbing. There are two accounts about how his crime was discovered. In one a mother shopping in a used clothing store discovered the handmade, one-of-a-kind dress she had used as a burial gown for her young daughter. The mother promptly brought this to the attention of the authorities. The other account is in Dale Morgan's *The Great Salt Lake*. He reports that George Clawson, the brother of 'Rone [Moroni] Clawson, decided to rebury his brother in the family plot. Upon opening the exhumed coffin, he found his brother was wearing no clothes. Further investigation showed 'Rone had been buried in clothes purchased at the personal expense of one of the city police officers. The trail led to Baptiste who was arrested while digging graves at the cemetery.[1] It was subsequently discovered that Baptiste (also called "John the Baptist") had been robbing graves for many years and that his small home was stacked with cartons containing clothing of the dead—especially that of women and children.

Judge Elias Smith heard the case, but it is not clear who pronounced the sentence. Brigham Young commented on the sentence from the tabernacle pulpit.[2] Baptiste was first transported to Antelope Island, where it was assumed he would die of starvation or exposure, but low water levels prompted fears he might escape. He was then transferred to Fremont Island, also in the Great Salt Lake. Some say his ears were cut off, "Grave Robber" branded on his forehead, and a ball and chain attached to his ankle.[3]

With punishment like this, the death penalty was probably not necessary. There were, of course, other forms of punishment available—official and unofficial—as means of social control. These included public confessions, excommunication, and ostracism. Most of these were intended to follow the early colonial philosophy of humiliation and ridicule. Still there were nine executions between 1847 and 1878.

* * *

The first two officially executed men were native Americans. Allen Weeks, a farmer living in Cedar Valley in present-day Utah County, sent his two sons, William F. and Warren D., up the canyon with an ox team for a load of poles. On 8 August 1854 a small band of about ten or twelve Ute Indians, who had separated from their tribe, camped near Cedar Valley. They swore among themselves that they would not make peace with whites until they had revenged certain wrongs of the previous year.

The Utes waited at the mouth of a canyon where inhabitants of Cedar Valley went for wood and poles. When the Weeks brothers came along with their ox team, the Indians killed and scalped them and mutilated their bodies. When the boys did not return home that night, a search party soon found the bodies. Friendly Indians, who had witnessed the crime and feared revenge, captured two of the Indians responsible for the murders and took them over to the authorities.[4]

Hosea Stout calls the death of the Indians "the first execution ever had in the Territory of Utah."[5] The record of the District Court credits the crime to the Devil:

> The Grand Jurors for the United States and the Territory of Utah and Salt Lake County . . . on there oaths do present and find . . . That two certain Indians usually called Long Hair and Antelope, late of the County of Utah in the Territory aforesaid on the eighth day of August A.D. one Thousand eight-hundred and fifty-four without the fear of God before there eyes moved, seduced and instigated by the Devil did then and there without the fear of God before there eyes upon the bodies of William F. Weeks and Warren D. Weeks, two human beings then and there being in the peace of God make an assault with two deadly weapons commonly called guns which said guns as aforesaid were loaded with powder and two leaden bullets each then and there held in the hands of the said Long Hair and Antelope indians as aforesaid and the said Long Hair and Antelope indians as aforesaid did then and there willfully, Feloniously and with Malice aforethought did shoot Wound Kill and Murder the said William F. Weeks and Warren D. Weeks.[6]

The witnesses listed for this hearing were Allen Weeks, Natsab, Yantan, and White Weasel. Another name, possibly Inon F. Itch, is illegible.

The Indians died in a double execution by hanging at the Jordan River Bridge in Salt Lake County. Stout wrote in his journal, "There was not a very large company of spectators present from the fact that the place of their execution was kept secret untill the procession started with the two Indians."[7]

* * *

Five years later, when working as a shoemaker for Alexander Carpenter, Thomas N. (or A. or H.) Ferguson asked for past wages and was refused. According to Ferguson, he went to a nearby saloon and had a "couple" of drinks. The next thing he remembered was sitting in jail charged with the murder of Carpenter, who had been shot on 17 September 1859. Ferguson had been in Utah just over a year at the time of his execution. Little is known about him other than the personal references he made in his final comments while standing on the gallows. He was twenty-seven years old and had no past history of crime.

His trial was over quickly. He appeared before Judge Charles E. Sinclair, who left the territory and returned East shortly after Ferguson's trial. Bill Hickman was appointed Ferguson's attorney. Found guilty, Ferguson was sentenced to be hanged on a Sunday, but Ferguson appealed to newly appointed territorial governor Alfred Cummings and the execution was rescheduled for Friday, October 28.

On the day of his execution, Ferguson was driven through town from the jail on West Second South to the city wall near Fifth East and South Temple.[8] He was sitting on his coffin in the back of a wagon as the procession moved along the north bench and halted about a quarter mile past the cemetery gate. As he mounted the scaffold he was asked if he had any final statement. Some accounts claim he talked for as much as four to eight hours. However, most accounts indicate he spoke less than an hour. The *Deseret News,* 2 November 1859, printed his comments about Judge Sinclair:

> Well, I was tried by the statutes of Utah Territory, which gives a man the privilege of being shot, beheaded or hanged; but was it given to me? No, it was not. All Judge Sinclair wanted was to sentence some one to be hanged, then he was willing to leave the Territory; and he had too much whiskey in his head to know the day he sentenced me to be executed on, and would not have known, if it had not been for the people of Utah laughing at him; it would have been Sunday. A nice Judge to send to any country.

After finishing, he asked that a prayer be said. Henry Jacobs, one of the guards, kneeled on the scaffold with Ferguson and offered a prayer. Ferguson's last words were, "Gentlemen, I bid you all farewell." Nearly 3,000 people were in attendance. After he was pronounced dead, Ferguson was buried near the scaffold where he was hanged. The *Valley Tan* ran these comments on 3 November 1859:

> Executed on Friday last, about one o'clock near the wall on the north side of this city. . . . greater consideration for the unfortunate man who was about to suffer, would have been evinced by taking some other direction to the gallows than the one pursued by those conducting him, even if they desired to witness his execution. The execution of Ferguson, we have been informed, is the first that has ever taken place in this Territory by a regular judicial sentence. Of the many murders that have taken place here, the perpetrators of them have in all instances escaped, or no notice whatever has been taken of their crime, the general belief being, that they were authorized or commanded by those who wield a despotic power over the lives and actions of the deluded and fanatical people that dwell in this Territory. And although we do not participate in the

> misguided sympathy of some of our citizens, who would have shielded Ferguson, had it been in their power, from the consequences of his crime, because he was a "gentile," we yet cannot help thinking that his fate would have been different if he had been a professed "Mormon."

* * *

On 31 July 1861, Robert Brown, a watchmaker, died of a gunshot wound to the chest. Witnesses said William Cockroft shot at Brown with a double barrelled shotgun as Brown passed his house. After missing with the first round, Cockroft rested the gun on the gate and as Brown raised his hand and said, "Don't shoot," Cockroft fired again. Brown died forty-five minutes later.

Not much is known about Cockroft—not even the spelling of his name which appears in various accounts as Cowcroft, Colcroft, Cockcroft, and Cockrof. The dispute was apparently a quarrel over irrigation water, no small matter in the arid west. In his diary Charles L. Walker refers to the incident by stating, "This morning two men got to quarreling about the water for irrigation, when one by the name of Cowcroft or Colcroft or some such name shot the other with a double barrel[e]d shot gun, and he died in about half an hour. I think the deceased was named Brown, a watch maker."[9]

On 13 September Cockroft was found guilty of first degree murder by a Salt Lake jury. According to the 25 September edition of the *Deseret News*, when asked if he had anything to say before sentencing, he replied: "I do not think I could benefit myself if I were to talk till tomorrow. I see which way the tide goes, and it is no use talking. I guess, judge, I will have to take what you have to lay upon my shoulders." He was the first sentenced to death by firing squad. He was executed the next Saturday, 21 September, between two and five in the afternoon. The *Deseret News* also commented that he was executed within the court house enclosure "to the disappointment of a few hundred persons who were anxiously waiting in the street for the prisoner to be brought out and taken to some place outside the city, where it was supposed he would be executed in a public manner."

* * *

Jason R. Luce was the first Mormon to be formally executed. On 7 December 1863, Luce attacked and stabbed Samuel R. Bunton with a bowie knife at the door of the Townsend Hotel at the corner of First South and West Temple in downtown Salt Lake City. He nearly severed Bunton's head. According to the *Union Vendetta,* 11 December 1863, after the killing Luce "brandished his bloody weapon in the air for nearly a quarter of an hour, acknowledging the deed, and apparently gloating over his triumph."

Luce said he had met Bunton in Bannock, Montana, while working at the mines. He was invited by Bunton to his home for supper. While there Bunton asked Luce if he was a Mormon and when he replied he was, Bunton jumped him, beating and stabbing him. On another occasion, Luce reported encountering Bunton, who drew a knife and threatened him. On 7 December Luce saw Bunton in downtown Salt Lake. He approached him, asked if he was Samuel R. Bunton, and when the man replied, "Yes," Luce said, "Well, we have an account to settle, and may as well settle it right here." Luce claimed Bunton then went for his weapon and Luce stabbed and killed him with his bowie knife.

There is more to the story than this, however. Jason Luce was a brother-in-law of Bill Hickman and a member of his gang. There were suspicions that this group did the bidding of those in positions of authority (ecclesiastical and secular) but also often ventured forth on their own. Sometime during 1859, Luce killed Joe Rhodes by running him through with a bowie knife. He was tried and acquitted. In the spring of 1862 he was arrested as a member of a group who beat Governor Dawson at Ephraim Hanks's way station as he was leaving the territory.[10] Luce and others involved in the beating claimed they were ordered to do so by law enforcement officials in the city.

With Hickman as his attorney, Luce was found guilty and sentenced to die by firing squad for Bunton's death. The sentence was carried out on 12 January 1864 at 12:00 p.m., exactly thirty-six days after the crime occurred.

Toward the end Luce turned against Hickman. On the day of his execution he was described as "cool, calm and collected." In a brief address he talked about the influence of "evil associates" and castigated those who "had betrayed him," indicating his "desire to brand [them] before the world." Brigham Young's secretary wrote: "Jason Luce executed at noon. His mother, brother [John Martin Luce], wife and five children visited him last night and this morning. He requested his brother to take care of a woman he had impregnated. He confessed all his sins and asked God for forgiveness. He addressed the people from his chair—feet manacled—pronounced Wm Hickman his betrayer, he bid the people goodby. His face was covered, 5 balls shot into his heart—no groan."[11]

The *Daily Vendetta,* 13 January 1864, concluded its coverage of Luce's execution with the following: "It is hoped that the awful doom of Luce will have a beneficial effect upon the community, and that the bloodthirsty will restrain their arm when passion, or still more unworthy motives, may impel to deeds of violence and crime. Truly, 'the way of the transgressor is hard.'"

On 2 October 1866 at Faust's overland station in Tooele County, Frederick White, a discharged soldier belonging to Company F of the Nevada Cavalry, fought with Robert Sutton, a hostler at the station. Sutton got the better of the argument, but he was angry at the offensive name White called him. That night he found White and shot him as he was sleeping in the wagon box. Sutton was tried and sentenced to death.

Sutton was a native of Fairfax Court House, Virginia. He came west approximately six years before this crime. After being sentenced to death, he was put into leg irons and manacles. He was kept in a small house on the west side of Main and Vine streets since Tooele had no jail. Sheriff John Gillespie (my great-grandfather) was given responsibility for the execution. A local carpenter built a coffin for Sutton, and he was transported in a wagon, atop his coffin, with a "red, white and blue rosette . . . pinned to the left breast of his shirt over his heart."[12]

Sheriff Gillespie describes the execution:

> Early in the morning, I pitched a small tent up on the bench, and had five men with rifles, four of them loaded with bullets and one loaded with powder, neither of the men knew who had the blank gun. I called out a company of cavalry to keep back the crowd of people, from all over the county. I set the prisoner on a chair about sixty yards from the mouth of the tent and covered his face and opened the front of the tent, and gave the word of command, and he was shot dead; we had his grave dug and buried him right there, and moved the tent and the men that night so that no one knew who did the shooting.[13]

Sutton's last words were, "To hell with your little Jesus." He then asked for a drink of whiskey. At the command to fire one report noted, "All but one of the people in Tooele heard the echoing reports of the shots that rang through the valley. The only one who failed to hear the crack of the rifles was Sutton who slumped lifeless against the bonds."[14] Sutton's execution took place exactly eight days after his crime.

On 11 December 1868 eighteen-year-old Chauncey W.

Millard was traveling along the west side of Utah Lake in the company of Harlem P. Swett and Chauncey Mayfield—both freighters. Swett and Mayfield were riding in the front seat and Millard was in the back of the wagon. Suddenly Millard fired from the back, killing Swett. He next shot Mayfield through the hand as Mayfield put up his hand to protect himself. Mayfield then jumped from the wagon and ran towards Lehi for help. Millard ran the other direction—making his escape toward Cedar Valley. For five days he holed up in a cabin, then robbed the owner, and disappeared again. He was captured 17 December by Orrin Porter Rockwell and Deputy Sheriff Henry Heath.

Millard was sentenced to be executed by firing squad. On 29 January, fifty days after his crime, he was led in irons to the west side of the Utah County court house in Provo. According to the *Deseret News,* 3 February 1869, four hundred persons were present. Prior to his execution he stood and read from the seventh chapter of Matthew, spoke briefly with officials, including the attending physician, and then sat down. The signal was given to fire and Millard was dead.

In the crowd was Orrin Porter Rockwell who had been involved in capturing Millard. Harold Schindler, Rockwell's biographer, wrote: "Whether he heard Millard's last conversation with the sheriff and the physician is not known, but it would have startled even the implacable Rockwell to know the boy had sold his body to the Provo surgeon for a pound of candy . . . and was eating the sweets at the moment the shots ended his life."[15]

Millard was one of the youngest persons executed in Utah. He came to Utah from New York where he had learned to survive on the streets and in the slums. The motive for this killing is not clear. Prior to his execution a writer for the *Deseret News* interviewed him and reported on 18 December 1868, "He seems utterly indifferent about his position. He says he has tried to make money by stealing and killing and having failed, would sooner die than live." Prison records have a small note, handwritten, to the side of his name: "He killed for pleasure."

* * *

In 1857 a wagon train of men, women, and children from Missouri and Arkansas was traveling through Utah on its way to California. After the expulsion of Mormons from Missouri and the killing of Parley P. Pratt, a Mormon apostle, in Arkansas by the estranged husband of one of Pratt's plural wives, there had been considerable animosity among many Mormons to anyone from that part of the country. Apparently there were other difficulties with this wagon train as it moved through Utah.

While camped at Mountain Meadows, Utah, the wagon train was attacked and ninety to one hundred twenty people were killed—the only survivors were seventeen young children. The massacre was at first attributed to Indians, but it was later discovered that as many as fifty Mormons were also involved. The only person ever prosecuted was John D. Lee. Some have suggested that Lee was the scapegoat for the incident; others have maintained that Brigham Young, attempting to secure statehood for Utah, was pressured to resolve the Mountain Meadows Massacre issue as expeditiously as possible.

Lee had left southern Utah after the massacre and settled on the Colorado River at a crossing known as Lee's Ferry. In 1874 while visiting in Panguitch, Utah, he was arrested. His first trial in 1875 resulted in a hung jury. The jury consisted of eight Mormons and four non-Mormons. He was tried again in 1876 by an all Mormon jury and was found guilty and sentenced to death. His comment at the time was, "I have been sacrificed in a cowardly, dastardly manner." After spending a year in prison, he was returned to Mountain Meadows. As the firing squad was being readied, his final words were, "Center on my heart boys. Don't mangle my body." When he was shot, his body fell backwards into the

"Center on my heart boys. Don't mangle my body." John D. Lee executed on 23 March 1877. Courtesy Utah State Historical Society.

John D. Lee sitting on his coffin at the site of the Mountain Meadows Massacre just before being executed by firing squad. Courtesy Utah State Historical Scoiety.

coffin he was sitting on. He was buried in Panguitch, Utah, by his sons.

LDS president David O. McKay reinstated Lee to full membership in the church in 1961. This reinstatement followed the persistent efforts of Ettie Lee, his granddaughter, and Juanita Brooks, author of *Mountain Meadows Massacre.*[16] Lee had organized group homes for delinquent boys in memory of her grandfather.

* * *

On 11 June 1877 Wallace Wilkerson and William Baxter were playing cribbage for money at James Hightower's saloon and store in Homansville, about three miles from Eureka near Tintic. An argument broke out, with each accusing the other of cheating. Wilkerson became angry, drew his pistol, and shot Baxter in the head. Then, according to witnesses, he took hold of Baxter's head and shot him again, this time in the side of the head. Wilkerson was caught soon afterwards and taken to Goshen, where he had to be protected from lynching.

Wilkerson was raised Mormon by his parents but had followed his own path. He had been born in Quincy, Illinois, and came to Utah with his parents at the age of eight. From the age of seventeen on he worked at tending stock, breaking horses, and other such jobs throughout the western states—even enlisting as a drummer in the military in San Francisco. His record contains reenlistments as well as several desertions. He travelled back and forth between Utah, California, and Nevada, but just before Baxter's killing he had returned to Payson, Utah, to be near his aging parents.

It was while working with his brothers in Homansville that he came in contact with Baxter. There had been trouble previous to the card game. Wilkerson recalled: "During this time I had been called a wild boy and a California Mormon. I guess you know what that is as well as I do; it's a slur" (Salt Lake Herald, 17 May 1879). A fight broke out during a dance at Baxter's saloon in Eureka. Wilkinson's narrative continues:

> Just then some jig dancing was done and a fellow named Gillespie got shooting off his mouth about being the best dancer. . . . So I invited him to dance with me. They had just commenced, when Gillespie said, ". . . I'm not going to dance with you, you son of a b——h." I told him to go slow or I'd teach him an entirely new waltz if he talked like that again. . . . Baxter ran in with a six-shooter in his hand, and said, "You G-d d——d Mormon son of a b——h, I heard you were coming here to make a row, and now we'll give you plenty" (ibid.).

From that time on, according to Wilkerson, there was constant conflict between the two men, culminating in the fight that ended Baxter's life in the Homansville saloon.

Wilkerson was found guilty and sentenced to die. His attorneys took the case to the U.S. Supreme Court where his appeal was rejected in October 1878. A reporter who visited with him while he was awaiting execution saw in Wilkerson proof for the validity of phrenology:

> In all the annals of criminals we know of no cranium or physiology which gives better proof of an innate criminal than those of our subject. His whole physique bore testimony to the truth of science of phrenology. He was wanting in ideality and imagination. This want saved him from the anguish that a sensitive person would have suffered in his situation–the certain approach of a felons doom. . . . So his wants were supplied, he could be merry over his coffin (*Salt Lake Tribune,* 17 May 1879).

On May 15 he left the prison and was transported to Provo where he spent the night. His wife had come from Tintic to be with him. The next day around twelve he was taken to the jail yard and a paper target was pinned to his heart. He had requested no blindfold and apparently was not tied to the chair: "The instant the bullets struck him, he raised on his feet, turned partially to the south, and as he was pitching forward, took two steps and fell on his left side on the ground. On the instant of striking the ground he turned on his face, exclaiming, 'My God! My God! they've missed it'" (ibid.). Apparently at the command to fire, Wilkerson drew his shoulders back, and this raised the paper target pinned to his jacket. Three bullet holes were found in the target, but they were an inch above his heart. The fourth bullet hit Wilkerson's left arm, six inches from the others (ibid.). Wilkerson lay on the ground fifteen minutes before he died, and officials briefly feared they would have to shoot him again. This spectacle prompted the Ogden editorial calling for the use of the guillotine for future executions.

NOTES

1. Dale L. Morgan, *The Great Salt Lake* (Indianapolis: Bobbs-Merrill, 1947), 274-330.

2. See *Journal of Discourses*, 26 vols. (Liverpool: Latter-day Saints' Book Depot, 1855-86), 9:191-94.

3. See Morgan, 278.

4. James B. Hill, "History of Utah State Prison, 1850-1952," M.A. thesis, Brigham Young University, 1952, 26-27.

5. Juanita Brooks, ed., *On the Mormon Frontier: The Diary of Hosea Stout*, 2 vols. (Salt Lake City: University of Utah Press, Utah State Historical Society.), 2:527.

6. Record of U.S. District Court #879, United States v. Longhair and Antelope.

7. Brooks, 2:527.

8. In *Deseret News Magazine*, 5 Aug. 1951.

9. A. Karl Larson and Katharine Miles Larson, eds., *Diary of*

Charles Lowell Walker, 2 vols. (Logan: Utah State University Press, 1980), 1:191.

10. For more information on this incident, see Hickman's autobiography, *"Brigham's Destroying Angel"* (Salt Lake City: Shepard Publishing Co., 1904), 149-59; Hope A. Hilton, *"Wild Bill" Hickman and the Mormon Frontier* (Salt Lake City: Signature Books, 1988), 100.

11. Hilton, p. 108.

12. Pearl Nelson Gillespie, "Tooele's One and Only Execution," paper read 2 Nov. 1970, Emma J. Atkin Camp, Daughters of Utah Pioneers.

13. *History of John Gillespie (Mar. 27, 1830-Feb. 9, 1915), Utah Pioneer,* Sept. 10, 1852. Compiled and Written by Himself (N.p.; n.d.), copy in my possession.

14. Pearl Nelson Gillespie.

15. Harold Schindler, *Orrin Porter Rockwell: Man of God, Son of Thunder* (Salt Lake City: University of Utah Press, 1966), 349.

16. Juanita Brooks, *John Doyle Lee: Zealot–Pioneer Builder–Scapegoat,* 2d ed. (Glendale, CA: Arthur H. Clark Co., 1962), 376.

4.

DOMESTIC STRIFE AND LAW OFFICIALS

By 1887 Mormon versus non-Mormon hostilities were passing. The territory, moving toward statehood, was no longer politically isolated. It was a time of tremendous economic growth and expansion as well as great mobility.

Twenty-two executions took place during the forty years from 1887 to 1926. Many of these involved foreign immigrants, and during this period Utah's first black was executed. Most of these executions resulted from crimes involving burglary or the murder of a spouse. Also for the first time, men were executed for killing law officers.

* * *

On 3 July 1880 nineteen-year-old Frederick Hopt killed young John F. Turner near Park City, Utah. Turner was the son of Sheriff John W. Turner of Utah County, who was also Provo City marshal. Hopt had previously been arrested in Provo by Sheriff Turner, who subsequently gave him money and helped him find a job.

On 28 June John Turner left for Park City with two spans

of horses to find work. On 1 July he joined up with Fred Hopt and Jack McCormick, who was traveling under the alias Jack Emerson. When last seen on 3 July Turner was driving one team of horses and Hopt the other. Turner's body was found on 11 July. Someone had killed him with an ax, rolled the body in a tent, covered it with large rocks, and tried to burn it. Hopt was pursued and arrested in Cheyenne, Wyoming, by Sheriff Turner.

At the time of his arrest, Hopt was asked why he killed the sheriff's son. He replied, "Turner was Sheriff and Johnny used to come to feed me at the jail and one morning he abused me, and I done it to get even with him" (*Salt Lake Tribune,* 12 Aug. 1887). Later Hopt blamed the killing on McCormick.

On the way back from Hopt's capture in Cheyenne, the train stopped in Rawlins, Wyoming, where a mob had gathered to lynch him—provided the sheriff turn away. He refused to do so. The same thing happened again as the train passed through two other towns. Each time, the victim's father asked those waiting to let the law take its course.

McCormick was sentenced to life in prison. He served five years and was pardoned by Governor Eli H. Murray—the last official act by the governor before leaving office.

Hopt was tried four times over seven years before he was found guilty and sentenced to death. He was executed on 11 August 1887 after giving his few possessions to fellow inmates and telling them goodbye. After leaving a request with the prison physician that his body not be used for medical purposes but buried outside the prison walls, he faced the firing squad without a blindfold. His last statement was: "Gentlemen, I have come to meet my fate. Had justice been done at my first trial, I would not be here today for this purpose. I have no ill-will toward any man living, and am prepared and ready to meet my God" (*Salt Lake Tribune,* 12 Aug. 1887).

At Hopt's request Sheriff Turner was not allowed to view

the execution. He saw the body afterwards and expressed satisfaction that justice had been done.

* * *

After twenty years of marriage, nine children, and numerous quarrels and fights, Enoch Davis killed his wife and buried her body in a potato hill near their home in Ashley, Utah. Davis claimed his wife had been unfaithful and he knew she was going to leave him. In a confession, he later stated, "I made up my mind that I would rather kill her and take the consequences than to have her leave me, and I did" (*Salt Lake Tribune*, 15 Sept. 1894).

At first Davis told his children their mother had run off. Later he told one of the older sons that she had committed suicide, "She died like a lady and I buried her like a gentleman." The son was suspicious and informed authorities who tracked Davis down and brought him to trial.

At his trial, his own children testified against him. Davis was actually sentenced to die three times before his execution on 14 September 1894. The *Salt Lake Tribune* reported his execution the next day: "Enoch Davis is dead. He died like a dog; in fact, the most despicable, mangy canine whelp that ever met an ignominious fate could not have whined itself out of existence in a more deplorable, decency-sickening state than was Enoch Davis's last hour."

He was taken by wagon from the prison at Sugarhouse to Dry Canyon near Lehi. Present at the execution were his brother, James Davis, and two of Enoch's sons, Berlden, seventeen, and Archie, fourteen. After talking briefly with his sons, he called out asking if there weren't "some prostitutes on the ranch." The *Tribune* reported on 15 September that "The deep blush of shame fell upon the whole party. What little sympathy, if any, there had been for the old man, was then and there lost, and many turned away in disgust."

Six guns were used in the firing squad. All were loaded. Four hit the small target drawn on a prescription blank by the doctor. After the execution his body was returned to the

"He died like a dog." Enoch Davis executed on 14 September 1894.

prison, where it was buried in the prison graveyard.

* * *

Charles Thiede was also executed for murdering his wife. On 1 May 1894, Mary Frank Thiede was found dead. Her throat had been cut at their residence located one hundred fifty yards from the saloon they owned on the outskirts of Murray, Utah. When the doctor arrived, her body was placed on the billiard table in the saloon while a search was made for the murder weapon. Her husband claimed he had been sleeping in the saloon, that men from the nearby army barracks had killed her or perhaps she had committed suicide.

Thiede, a German immigrant, one of eighteen children including four pairs of twins, had lived in Utah for about eight years. He owned and operated several saloons and roadhouses known as "tough places" throughout the area. He and his wife had a nine-year-old daughter named Annie. Prior to his execution he made out a will leaving all of his property to her. She was later adopted by a Mrs. Koenen, Thiede's spiritual advisor in the Church of Christ Scientist while he was awaiting execution.

The hanging took place at the county jail in Salt Lake City. Many thought it would be at the prison, but the sheriff considered it too difficult to transport the heavy gallows apparatus that far. Thiede's was the first execution since Utah achieved statehood, and the state tried a new method of hanging. The hanged man was jerked upwards by a counterweight rather than allowed to drop.

As Thiede approached the platform, his final words were: "Gentlemen—I am convicted of murdering my wife. For the last time before dying, I wish to profess my innocence" (*Salt Lake Herald,* 8 Aug. 1896). At the signal, the weight was dropped and Thiede's body was lifted into the air where he dangled and was declared dead after fourteen minutes—his death resulted from strangulation as his neck had not been broken.

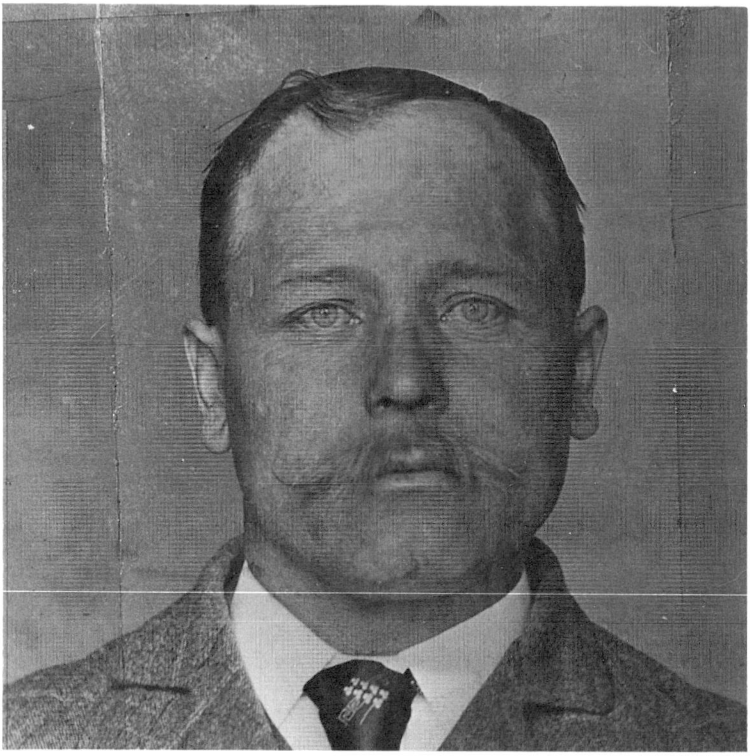

"First execution after statehood." Charles Thiede executed on 7 August 1896.

Thiede was buried in the Sandy City cemetery. Four deputy sheriffs served as pall bearers and, to fulfill Thiede's last request, he was promised that his wife's body would eventually be relocated next to his.

* * *

Patrick Coughlin and Fred George began their crime spree in Park City stealing berries. Things escalated when they stole a horse to facilitate their escape after the sheriff began to pursue them. They stopped for the night at Palmer's cabin near Echo Canyon, where they were surrounded by lawmen during the night. At daybreak the lawmen opened fire on the cabin.

During the shooting, two officers were killed. N. E. Dawes of Evanston was killed when Coughlin and George returned fire, and Thomas Stagg of Echo was killed in the crossfire of the other officers. Coughlin and George escaped down Ogden Canyon to City Creek in Salt Lake City and then on to Tooele. They were captured near Grantsville. Returned to Randolph for trial, both were found guilty—Coughlin sentenced to be executed and George to life imprisonment.

Little is known of Coughlin. He was apparently a resident of Park City. His mother travelled from there to Randolph to spend a few hours with her son the night before his execution. She took his body back to Park City to be buried. The *Salt Lake Tribune,* 16 December 1896, described a supposed incident from his childhood: "'Patsy, my boy,'" the city marshal of Park City often said, 'You want to put on the brakes, or you'll find yourself in a tight box someday.' 'Not on your life,' the irresponsible Patsy would warble, after which he would swagger down the street in quest of some new form of deviltry."

The *Ogden Standard-Examiner,* 18 December 1896, also made assertions about his past: "From his earliest childhood Coughlin exhibited traits of cruelty and hatred. Dumb animals were the victims of heartless pranks and neighbors' children suffered from his viciousness and abuse. When

"Life is too short to pick bones." Fred George and Patrick Coughlin photographed shortly after their arrest. Executed 15 December 1896 at Sage Hollow, Woodruff, Utah. Courtesy Charlie Trentleman and the *Ogden Standard-Examiner*.

Removal of Patrick Coughlin's body immediately after execution. Courtesy Charlie Trentleman and the *Ogden Standard-Examiner*.

asked how he wanted to be executed, he responded, 'I'll take lead.' When asked what he wanted to eat before his execution, he responded, '. . . I'd like to have a little Dawes or Stagg on toast,' referring to the two men killed."

He was executed by firing squad. Five rifles, one with a blank load, and another the one Coughlin used to kill Dawes, were fired. The *Herald* reported on 18 December 1896:

> No birds sang in the branches of the leafless trees; no hum of insects droned a farewell; no soft breezes fanned the condemned man's cheek or whispered him a word of hope from the waving shrubbery as might have been in summer time. On the contrary the landscape never looked more drear and the crunching now sounded harsh under the foot. The cold, raw and gusty wind seemed to shriek in glee as the soul of the dead mounted on the echoes of the rifle shots and winged its way to the eternal judge.

Fred George was pardoned because of his youth. (Stagg's wife believed, to the day she died, that it was the other officers who killed her husband in the cross-fire, not Coughlin.)

* * *

On Monday night, 17 December 1901, James R. Hay, secretary of the Pacific Lumber Company, was reported missing from his residence at 2211 Walnut Avenue in Salt Lake. It was reported that he had just received $3,800 in gold from Peter Mortensen, a local contractor, and that Hay had left Mortensen's home about 9:30 to turn the money over to George E. Romney, the company manager.

Hay's body was discovered several days later in a vacant lot near Mortensen's home. He had been shot in the head and the money was missing. Mortensen was arrested, tried for murder, and sentenced to death by firing squad. James Sharp, the father-in-law of the victim, testified in court to having received a revelation that Mortensen was the killer and that he had seen a trail of blood leading to his son's grave. Such unusual testimony concerned Joseph F. Smith, then president of the Mormon church:

> Recently a man charged with the murder of another man was examined before a committing magistrate in Salt Lake City. The father-in-law of the murdered man, during the examination on the part of the State, related a conversation had between himself and the accused soon after the commission of the crime. During the conversation, according to newspaper report, the father-in-law of the murdered man laid the crime at the door of the accused. In the cross-examination the attorney for the defendant pressed the witness as to how he knew that the accused was guilty of the crime. The reply, as given in the press, was, because God had revealed it to him. It does not appear from the further proceedings in the case that the testimony was excepted to or withdrawn, or that the magistrate informed the witness that such evidence was incompetent and could not be received. . . . [N]o member of the Church of Jesus Christ of Latter-day Saints should, for one moment, regard such testimony as admissible in a court of law, and to make the case perfectly clear it may be further stated that such evidence would not be permissible even in a Church court, where rules of evidence, though not so technical, are founded largely upon the same principles that govern the rules of evidence in a court of law. Any attempt, therefore, to make it appear that such evidence is in keeping with the tenets of the "Mormon" faith is wholly unjustified (in *Juvenile Instructor* 37 [15 Feb. 1902]:114).

On the day of his execution, Mortensen was visited by his father, two brothers, his sister-in-law, a young nephew, and his attorneys. He expressed to them a desire to be buried in the Ogden cemetery next to his mother and brother. (Ogden cemetery records do not show this ever occurred. Instead prison records identify Mortensen as being buried at the prison cemetery at Sugarhouse.)

Mortensen next met with reporters and praised his guards, the warden, and other officers involved in his case. At the conclusion of this meeting, the prison physician quietly asked if Mortensen wanted an opiate. He refused this as well as a cigar offered by one of the newspaper men: "I don't smoke." As he passed the cells of three other men awaiting execution, he said, "Good-bye boys . . . I hope you have better luck than I have."

Mortensen made a farewell statement to reporters: "To this world I want to say, and I swear by the heavens above, by the earth beneath, and by all that I hold near and dear on earth, that I am not guilty of that cowardly murder of my dearest friend. I ask, therefore, no man's pardon for aught that I have done in life. I am confident that my life is an example to most people." His last words, spoken just seconds before the command to fire, were: "I have nothing to say except that I am innocent."

The *Tribune* reported 21 November 1903 that "99 out of 100 people in Salt Lake" believe he died with a lie on his lips:

> Even when he could no longer doubt the feeling entertained toward him by the community, when his wife had deserted him, his brothers-in-law forsaken him, he kept up the sham. He never tired of parading his religion and holding himself up as a pattern of morality. The court, the jury, the witnesses, the Supreme Court, the Board of Pardons, the Governor might be wrong, but he, Peter Mortensen, was always right.

Mortensen's self-righteous attitude made him unpopular, even among other prisoners. While he was on death

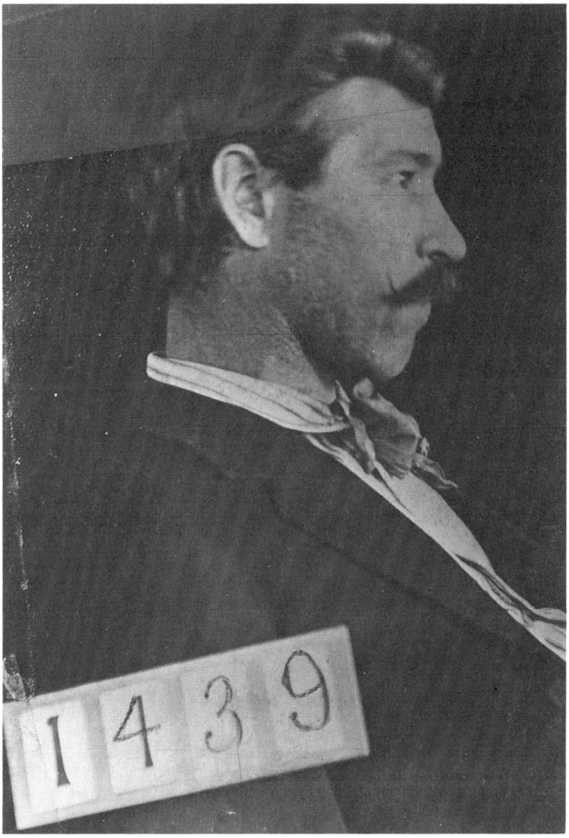

"A revelation showed him guilty of murder." Peter Mortensen executed on 20 November 1903.

Location of execution site along the south wall of Sugarhouse prison. Courtesy Utah State Historical Society.

row, an escape was engineered by several prisoners; they opened the cell of every man except Mortensen's.

As Mortensen entered the yard on the day of his execution, his eyes were covered with a handkerchief. He was placed in the chair and his ankles were tied to the lower rung. The *Tribune* described in detail the location of this execution, also the location of other executions conducted at the Sugarhouse prison:

> On the east side of the prison yard is a low brick building about 100 feet long north and south which is used as the prison blacksmith shop. Between this building and the east wall of the prison yard is a driveway about 50 feet wide. Well toward the south end of the building on the side facing the driveway and the east prison wall is a pair of double doors. The door[s] stood open yesterday and in their place hung a curtain made of common blue denim cloth. At about the height of a man's shoulder five round holes had been cut in this curtain at regular intervals across its width, and a foot or so higher other holes of irregular shape appeared. Behind this curtain were stationed the men who took Peter Mortensen's life at behest of the law, their identityknown only to the Sheriff and a very few of his trusted deputies.

Tickets had been distributed for spectators, and a large crowd gathered. After the signal to fire, Mortensen's body slumped forward and it was over. There was no smoke from the rifles as smokeless powder was used. After the execution souvenirs—chunks of the posts and fragments of the bullets—were made available to the officers. The same guns were used on Mortensen as had been used on Fred Hopt.

* * *

While lying in bed with his wife in Salt Lake City at 48 West Third South, Frank Rose had been talking about her "sporting around" and how it should be stopped. According to the *Salt Lake Tribune* (28 Dec. 1903), Rose said, ""Well, there's only one way to stop it, and that is for me to kill you." "All right!" she said, "I'm perfectly willing you should. I'm perfectly satisfied to die and quit this life. It's the only way I can stop it." Rose then took out his pistol, placed it behind her right ear, and pulled the trigger.

She remained conscious for more than an hour. Rose later said they talked together: "She asked me to put a wet towel around her head and rub the place where the bullet had entered. I did as she asked. Then she asked me to kiss her and I did so." The *Deseret News* (26 December 1903) goes on to report that she put her arm around her husband's neck

> and begged him to bring the baby to her. Blood was flowing freely from the wound and the sands of life were running rapidly. The hardened man placed the little one in his mother's arms. She kissed the baby while the latter patted her head affectionately. She asked Rose to leave the baby in her arms and the man lay down beside his wife and calmly watched her die.

Rose then left, went on a drinking binge, and two days later told the police he had killed his wife. He directed them to the apartment where they found two-year-old baby Elmer next to the body of his dead mother. The child had been there the entire time. As they entered, the baby said, "Mamma won't wake up; I can't make her" (Deseret News, 21 April 1904).

Rose made a full confession and awaited execution. He never expressed any regrets. When interviewed prior to his execution, he stated: "I have no regrets whatever. I feel sorry for my little baby but not for the woman. If I had it to do over again, I would do it." He believed in a form of predestination. Killing his wife and his eventual execution were

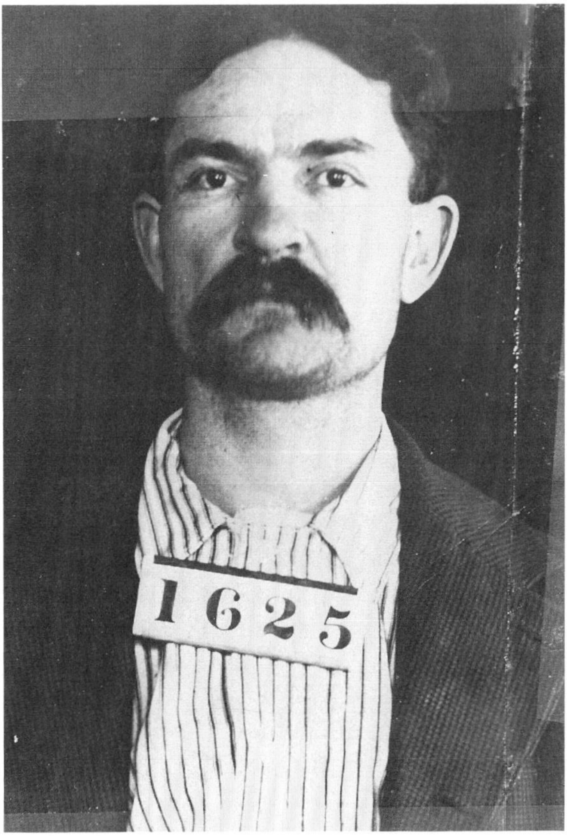

"I believe all of this was predestined." Frank Rose executed on 22 April 1904.

both a part of fate. Speaking to the warden, Rose stated: "I believe all of this was predestined and I could not help doing what I did. A power stronger than mine controlled me" (*Deseret News*, 21 April 1904). Rose also confessed to at least ten other murders.

For his last meal he ordered cherries, a cup of coffee, and some cake. In his last letter to his mother he wrote: "Dear Mother—I drop you these few lines to bid you my last farewell, and I want you to look upon my fate as for the best. I can blame no one now living for my condition. The one at fault has gone before, and I believe is at peace and rest" (*Deseret News*, 21 April 1904).

He died by firing squad 22 April 1904 before one hundred ten spectators and was buried in the prison cemetery. Rose's son, Elmer, went to live with his grandmother.

* * *

About 5:30 p.m. on 9 May 1911, J. J. Morris and John Murray (alias Mike Connors) robbed the Uncle Sam loan office at 30 East First South in Salt Lake City. After pocketing diamonds and jewelry, Morris and Murray made their escape. An alarm sounded as the two ran down Commercial Street to Orpheum Avenue, where they then turned east to State Street. They were pursued by a growing crowd of townspeople.

Reaching Second South they turned west toward Main Street. Just before reaching Main, Murray was stopped and struck on the head by a former policeman. Morris continued, reaching Commercial Street and running across Second South. In front of Held's Pawn Shop at the southeast corner of Second South and Main Street, a young man named Joseph Walter Axtell grabbed him by the shoulder and tried to hold him. Morris pushed his revolver into Axtell's stomach and pulled the trigger, killing him. Morris was then subdued by a deputy sheriff and other officers. It was all they could do to keep the angry crowd from killing Morris.

Morris never gave his real name in order to protect his parents. After a quick trial he was sentenced to be executed. His partner, John Murray, received a life sentence. During the trial and in a prepared statement just before his execution, Morris accused Salt Lake City police of stealing diamonds and other jewels from him at the time of his arrest. These, he said, had been sewed in the lining of his vest. The charges were investigated but never substantiated.

At his sentencing, Morris chose to be hanged. It was reported that he did this to cause the state the greatest inconvenience (only four other men had been hanged previous to this). His own statement, however, gave another reason: "I do not want to meet Axtell on the way. He died by the bullets so I don't want to die that way. That's why I chose hanging instead of shooting" (*Deseret News,* 27 April 1912).

On the last Sunday before his execution, as a form of repentance, Morris sent the following note, printed in the *Tribune,* 30 January 1912, to the father of his victim:

> Mr. Axtell—Dear Sir:
>
> I do not doubt but that you will be surprised upon receipt of this letter. But trust you will not feel offended, as I feel no vengeance against you or your family on account of this unfortunate affair. I cannot restore your son to you, but will do the best I can. If you feel that it will be of any benefit to you to see me executed and you cannot gain admission to the prison at the time of execution, and you will inform me on or before Monday morning I am allowed by law to use five invitations, and will cheerfully reserve one for your admission. Trusting this will cause you no unnecessary worry, I beg to remain respectfully,
>
> J. J. Morris

Mr. Axtell was working out of town at the time, but his

wife indicated she had encouraged him not to attend and he had decided not to be there.

Morris spent the night before his execution telling jokes. One of them concerned two men about to be executed by hanging from a bridge over a turbulent stream. Morris said: "The first man slipped from the noose when he was swung off the bridge and fell into the water. He swam to the shore and escaped. When they started to swing the other fellow, he said: 'Now be sure and tie the knot tight, for I can't swim'" (*Salt Lake Tribune,* 30 April 1912).

On his way to the gallows he passed Jules Szirmay also awaiting execution. He called out, "Goodbye, I'll get the road ready for you down below" (*Salt Lake Tribune,* 30 April 1912). Three deputies each pulled tangled ropes—only one of which actually sprung the trap. Nine minutes after the drop Morris was pronounced dead.

For the first time in Utah, only one newspaper reporter was present at the execution. Previously representatives of the press had been appointed as special sheriff's deputies in order to comply with the law for witnesses at executions. In an attempt to stop what they considered the media's "lurid accounts" of executions, the Board of Corrections proposed a new plan: local newspapers would meet and agree on one reporter to represent all the newspapers and to "syndicate" a report, which would be submitted to a member of the board prior to release (*Deseret News,* 30 April 1912; *Salt Lake Herald-Republican,* 30 April 1912).

Morris had willed his body to the prison physician, Dr. H. Z. Lund, for scientific study. Lund's grandson later recounted in the *Utah Historical Quarterly* (35 [1962]: 31-36) what became of the body. His grandfather had reduced the corpse to a skeleton by boiling it in sulfur water and lime. The bones were stored in a wooden box and kept in the barn until after Lund's death in 1912. Five or six years later, Lund's grandson assisted by his grandmother, Lund's wife, buried the bones after wrapping them in old copies of the

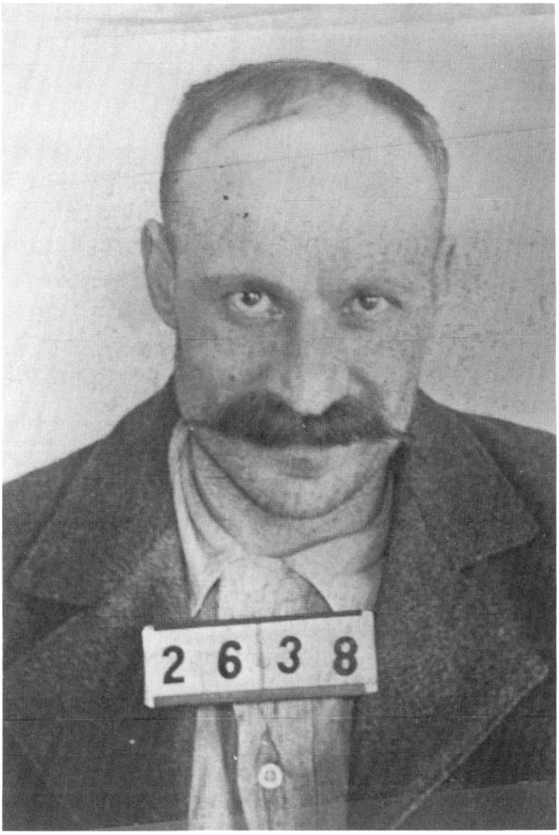

"Chose hanging so as not to meet his victims in the next life." J. J. Morris executed on 30 April 1912.

Mormon church's official magazine, the *Improvement Era*. They were buried in a barnyard on the block northwest of Temple Square.

* * *

On 12 October 1910 a fourteen-year-old boy, Thomas Karrick, was shot to death when he returned from school for lunch and surprised a burglar in his home at 150 South Thirteenth East in Salt Lake City. Despite an elaborate alibi, Jules C. E. Szirmay, a Murray distillery worker, was arrested, tried, and sentenced to death. The case against him was based on circumstantial evidence, and had Szirmay stuck to his original story when he appeared before the Board of Pardons, he may never have been executed. He claimed to have been in the Karrick house with a man named Joe. When the Karrick boy returned home unexpectedly, Szirmay heard him upstairs, climbed through a basement window, and ran from the house leaving Joe behind. He knew nothing that transpired after that.

Szirmay was born in Austria. He ran away from home, landed first in New York City in 1906, and from there went to Chicago, Omaha, San Francisco, Sacramento, and finally by freight car to Salt Lake City. He found employment near Murray at a distillery. He spent most of his time reading "scientific books," which he purchased from the proceeds of his petty thefts.

Prior to his execution and after being turned down by the Board of Pardons, he released a signed confession, which was printed in the *Salt Lake Telegram* (22 May 1912):

> I first entered the basement and, after going through the trunks there, I went upstairs on the second floor. . . . I was in the house about two hours, both up and downstairs.
>
> Coming from one of the upstairs rooms I saw the boy coming, and I rushed back into the room and seized two revolvers and rushed at him. I com-

"He killed for scientific books." Jules C. E. Szirmay executed on 22 May 1912.

menced firing from above.

He threw up his hands and said, "Please don't shoot me," but I fired and the first shot missed his head.

He turned slightly and I fired two shots quickly the second time, when he fell in a corner in a sitting posture with his head fallen forward on his arms. . . .

I am very sorry for what I did and can give no reason why I did it, other than in my excitement at being discovered I lost my head and did not realize what I was doing. I repeat that I am very sorry, but realize it is too late to undo the wrong I did. . . .

Jules C. E. Szirmay

Szirmay was executed by firing squad on 22 May 1912 in the same chair in which Frank Rose and Peter Mortensen were executed. He was buried at the prison.

* * *

Harry Thorne and Thomas Riley were the first pair to be executed since Antelope and Longhair in 1854. Thorne was also one of the youngest men executed in Utah, and Riley was the first to be executed who had not actually committed murder. On 24 March 1910, Thorne, Riley, and another man identified as "Red" entered the grocery store of George W. Fassell at 627 East Fourth South and told him to raise his hands. As he was complying, Thorne shot him. The three men emptied the cash register and left. Thorne and Riley were later captured, but Red was never caught.

Little is known of Thorne—not even his real name. Just before his execution he told prison warden Arthur Pratt his true name and mother's address so she could be notified, but Pratt never recorded it. He gave his body to a physician after his mother had been telegraphed in Cleveland, Ohio, and had responded that "she was in no position to dispose of the body" (*Salt Lake Herald-Republican,* 27 Sept. 1912).

Thorne had exhibited great interest in the two execu-

"Utah's youngest to be sentenced to die." Harry Thorne executed on 26 September 1912.

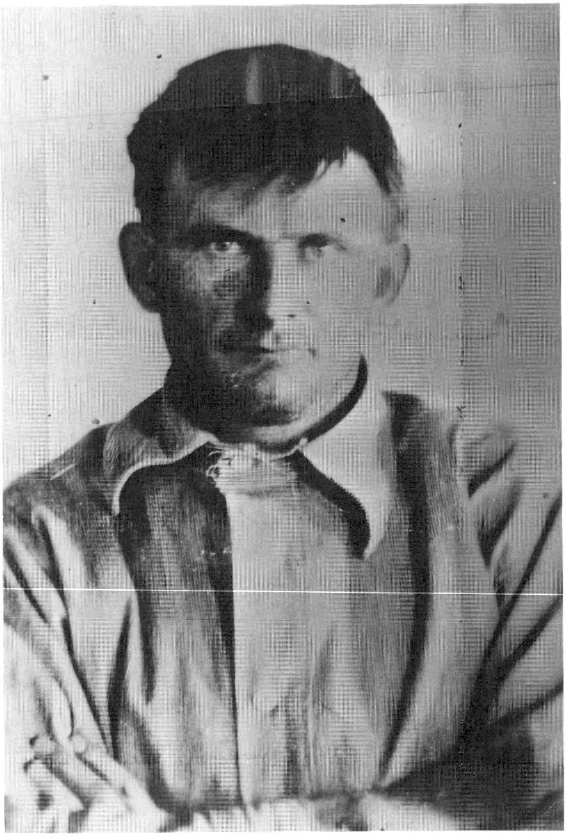

"Did not do the killing but was executed." Thomas Riley executed on 24 October 1912.

tions preceding his own. Of Morris and Szirmay, he asked, "Well, did he die like a man?" He requested that no newspaper reporters or others except the minimum necessary be present at his execution. Only thirteen men were there when the firing squad ended his life.

Riley's execution followed Thorne's by about four weeks. It was the fourth during a six-week period. Even so, the *Salt Lake Telegram* (24 Oct. 1912) voiced concern with the lengthy amount of time between crime and execution:

> Two years and seven months ago Thomas Riley committed the crime for which he was shot today. No wonder the public forgot what he was being shot for and cared less. . . . It is taken for granted that a man is shot or hanged not so the state may have its vengeance on the slayer, but that others with murder in their hearts may be so impressed with fear and dread of consequences that they will not kill. . . . And the legal machinery of the state is so clogged with delaying tactics that a man of any considerable age might kill and rest assured that by employing shrewd lawyers he could linger until natural death overtook him before the executioner had a chance to carry out his grim purpose.

Riley pleaded with Governor William Spry to commute his sentence because Thorne had actually fired the shots that killed Fassell, but his request was refused.

Only nine people witnessed Riley's execution. After being strapped in the chair, he raised his head and prayed while those present bowed their heads. His last hours had been given to prayer for forgiveness as he knelt on the floor next to his cot. "I am ready, gentlemen," were his last words.

* * *

At about 12:30 a.m. on 5 February 1911, Albert V. Jenkins and George Bentley, partners in a Sunnyside gambling

"Three times dreamed of his own execution." Frank Romeo executed on 20 February 1913.

house, left their place of business to go to Bentley's house about a hundred yards away. Jenkins was carrying $418 in gold and silver coin. As they approached the house they were accosted by three men who began firing at them. Bentley started to run but fell down, remaining there as though he had been shot. The men continued firing at Jenkins until he was dead. Later it was discovered that his throat had also been cut.

Three men were arrested for the crime—Frank Romeo, Robert Zaffy, and John Corier. Romeo and Zaffy were tried together. Corier was given a separate trial. Each attempted to implicate the other and exonerate himself. Corier was convicted but given a life sentence. Romeo and Zaffy were both sentenced to death by firing squad. Zaffy's sentence was commuted to life by the board of pardons the day before his scheduled execution. The board refused to commute Romeo's sentence, because he was the most culpable and he "did the most of the shooting, actually took the money from Jenkins, carried it some distance and then divided it with his partners in crime" (*Deseret News,* 20 Feb. 1913).

Romeo, an Italian miner, was executed at 8:00 a.m. in the Sugarhouse prison yard. The day before his execution he confessed to Governor William Spry in a private conversation. He did not expect commutation. He dreamed of his execution on three separate occasions and believed nothing could be done to save him. On the morning of his execution when the sheriff came to get him and asked if he was ready, Romeo called out, "No, I want my breakfast." His confessor, Father Vincent, requested that Romeo be given nothing to eat after midnight, so he was not fed. Before being taken forcibly from his cell, Romeo deeded his body to the prison physician. On the way across the yard he collapsed and had to be supported and dragged to the chair. Romeo was the fifth man to be executed in Utah within nine months.

* * *

On 10 January 1914 J. G. Morrison's grocery store at 778

South West Temple was robbed by two men. Morrison and his seventeen-year-old son, J. Arling Morrison, were shot and killed, but not before they fired at and apparently wounded one of the robbers. Morrison's other son, fourteen-year-old Merlin, was the only witness. The next day Joe Hill sought medical help for a gunshot wound. The police were notified and Hill was arrested. He claimed that he had been shot in an argument over a woman he was with the night before. When asked to name the woman, he refused, "lest her reputation be ruined." He was tried for the Morrison deaths, found guilty, and sentenced to die by firing squad.

Hill was a wandering song writer and member of the Industrial Workers of the World (IWW) or Wobblies. His execution has been one of the most widely publicized in Utah history. Letters of support for Hill came from all around the world. Great pressure was put on Utah's governor to stay the execution and commute the sentence. Hill's trial and execution took place during a period of labor conflict and union fever, when the IWW was active in trying to change the economic, political, and social structure of society.

The lyrics of one of Hill's songs describe the flavor of the times:

> Workers of the world, awaken
> Break your chains, demand your rights.
> All the wealth you make is taken
> By exploiting parasites.
> Shall you kneel in submission
> From your cradle to your graves
> Is the height of your ambition
> To be good and willing slaves?
> Chorus:
> Arise, ye prisoners of starvation!
> Fight for your own emancipation;
> Arise, ye slaves of every nation
> In one union grand.

Our little ones for bread are crying,
And millions are from hunger dying;
The end the means is justifying,
'Tis the final stand.

Rumors, charges, and counter charges were rampant throughout Hill's trial and execution. A number of factors may have influenced Hill's execution. Many in Salt Lake City were hostile toward the IWW. Hill seemed to have a naive faith that the justice system would find him innocent. Some accused the religious, political, or business establishment of framing Hill. Support for Hill by Virginia Snow Stephen, daughter of Mormon church president Lorenzo Snow, caused bitter controversy. From his cell, Hill wrote his last will in verse on the day before his 19 November 1915 execution:

My Last Will

My will is easy to decide
For there is nothing to divide
My kin don't need to fuss and moan
"Moss does not cling to a rolling stone."
My body?-Oh-if I could choose
I would to ashes it reduce
And let the merry breezes blow
My dust to where some flowers grow.
Perhaps some fading flower then
Would come to life and bloom again.
This is my Last and Final Will.
Good luck to all of you—
Joe Hill.

In a last letter to Bill Haywood, secretary of the IWW, Hill requested: "Goodbye Bill: I die like a true rebel. Don't waste any time mourning—organize! It is a hundred miles from

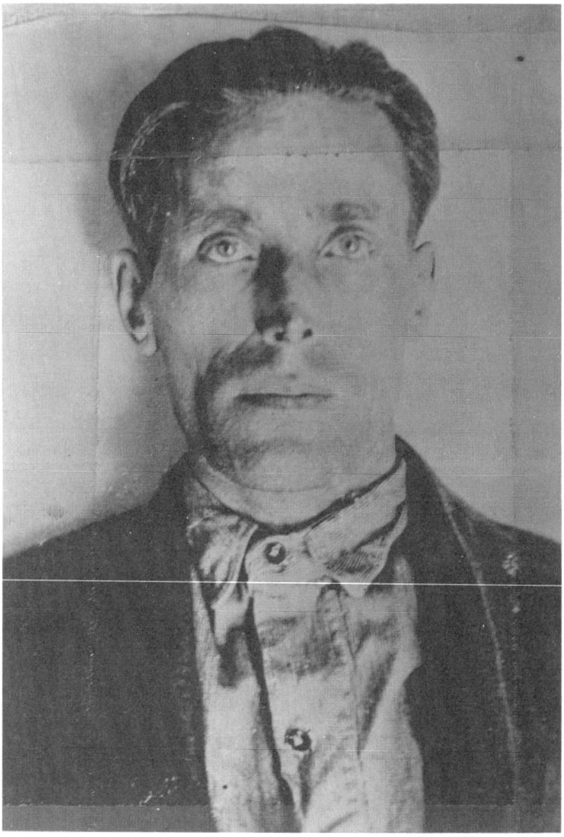

"I don't want to be found dead in Utah." Joe Hill executed on 19 November 1915.

here to Wyoming. Could you arrange to have my body hauled to the state line to be buried? I don't want to be found dead in Utah" (*Salt Lake Herald-Republican,* 19 Nov. 1915).

Hill himself gave the command to fire. One of the members of the firing squad described the execution:

> It seemed like shooting an animal. How my thoughts wandered! It seemed an age waiting for the command to fire. And then, when it came from Hillstrom himself, I almost fell to my knees. We fired. I wanted to close my eyes, but they stared at the white paper heart, scorched and torn by four lead balls. Four blackened circles began to turn crimson, then a spurt and the paper heart was red (*New York Tribune,* 20 Nov. 1915).

Hill was cremated and his ashes scattered throughout many foreign countries and all of the states except Utah.

* * *

Using the name D. C. Robbins, Howard DeWeese and his wife, Fanny Fisher DeWeese, rented an apartment at 455 1/2 South State in Salt Lake City. On the morning of 22 September 1916, her body was found in the apartment by the landlady. She had been killed with a flatiron twisted in a towel, and her face and head were mutilated. Her body went unidentified until a New York dentist recognized her bridgework. Then the murderer was sought.

Howard DeWeese was born in Ohio. His mother died when he was five years old, shortly after his father had moved the family to Canon City, Colorado. Two years later his father remarried. At the age of sixteen, Howard left home and began to live on his own. He was in and out of trouble, at one point suspected of a Seattle streetcar robbery and murder. DeWeese and his new wife came to Salt Lake in 1916, shortly after their marriage in Nevada. She had just left her first husband.

By the time authorities started looking for DeWeese, he had disappeared. He was not apprehended until he walked into a Chicago detective's office and surrendered. He claimed he was out committing a burglary at the time his wife was killed. They had been to the Orpheum Theater that evening and had noticed two strange men. Upon returning home he had gone out to commit a burglary, leaving his wife at home. In her possession were several thousand dollars worth of diamonds given her by her first husband. When DeWeese returned, he found his wife's body and, noticing her diamond earrings missing, set out immediately to track down the two strange men he believed to be her killers. According to his story, he found one of them and killed him by "thrusting a revolver into his mouth and discharging it" (*Salt Lake Tribune,* 24 May 1918).

Figuring prominently in his trial was the pair of earrings Mrs. DeWeese had been wearing at the time of her murder. DeWeese had written: "Those accursed earrings! The man who stole them killed my wife" (*Salt Lake Tribune,* 24 May 1918). The earrings were later discovered in a safety deposit box DeWeese had rented under the name of J. E. Warren. They were identified by the jeweler who had made them for Mrs. DeWeese's first husband. However, the diamonds had been removed. The discovery of these earrings prompted the state of Utah to bring charges against DeWeese for murder and robbery. DeWeese claimed he had recovered the earrings from the real murderer.

The trial got off to a strange start when one of the jurors died while eating lunch in a nearby cafe. Another juror was selected and DeWeese was subsequently found guilty. When asked if he had anything to say before sentencing, he asked what kind of guns would be used by the firing squad and seemed satisfied when assured they would be high-powered rifles.

His father, a well-to-do "civil engineer and fruit rancher," travelled from Canon City, Colorado, to appear before

"Those accursed earrings." Howard DeWeese executed on 24 May 1918.

the Board of Pardons and appeal for a commutation on his son's behalf. He was described as "a man of quiet dignity, on whom sixty years of hard life set lightly." Unable to sway the board, he returned to Colorado before the execution.

Prior to his execution, DeWeese was asked by reporters, "What has been mostly occupying your thoughts?" He responded:

> The absurdities and inconsistencies of life and people. I can't help smile when I think of the illogic with which people determine problems of life, and the unreasonableness of my being placed where I am. I don't consider the people who put me here intelligent and good enough for me to live in the same world with them. . . . I don't reason the same as other people. I'm different. I've had a different life. I'm an exception. I believe in good government, in doing right, but force of circumstances led me into the path I have taken. I've been nothing but a guttersnipe and hanger around back alleys all my life. But no man gets more pleasure out of life than I do, and I see the humor in my situation (*Salt Lake Tribune,* 24 May 1918).

When asked what was the last thing he wanted to say, he replied, "Tell 'em to go to hell."

DeWeese was executed on 24 May 1918. He had requested that a white silk handkerchief be placed under the target over his heart. After the execution he wanted the warden to send this to his dead wife's first husband. The handkerchief was pinned to his undershirt under the target but was never sent. The warden kept it as a relic at the state prison.

* * *

Austrian-born John Borich was arrested for the murder of Velma Adkins, whom he knew as Velma Green. They had met in Pioneer Park in Salt Lake City in July 1918. During their friendship she discovered an insurance brochure in his pocket and suggested he take out an insurance policy on her life so he could get the money if she died.

Her body was later found along the Lincoln Highway on the outskirts of Tooele. Borich claimed he was her husband and someone else had killed her. Later he confessed to the killing and said he had been urged to commit it by the woman's real husband. At last he confessed murdering her for the insurance money. He hoped to win back his own wife who left him "because he was unable to give her the finery that she craved" (*Salt Lake Tribune,* 18 Dec. 1919).

Borich was born and spent his childhood in the province of Dalmatia, Austria. He blamed his troubles on this fact. His wife, born in the United States but of English parents, taunted and quarrelled with him because he had been unable to get citizenship and was categorized as an "alien enemy." In the intense patriotism of World War I, she further insulted him by dating soldiers. According to Borich, "She told me she would come back to me if I had more money" (*Salt Lake Tribune,* 16 Dec. 1919).

After his arrest he claimed the idea of killing Mrs. Adkins had never entered his mind until after he had the insurance policy in his pocket. At her urging, they obtained the $2,000 ($4,000 in case of accidental death) insurance policy posing as man and wife and using the name of Mr. and Mrs. John Green. Mrs. Adkins had left a husband and two children in Twin Falls, Idaho, to come to Salt Lake. On 16 September 1918 while the two of them were walking along the highway, he strangled her, leaving her body in the middle of the road. Borich claimed not to have known the woman's real name until after her murder.

Prior to his execution, he indicated he had not heard from his mother or sisters in Austria since war broke out: "I would not want my mother to know of this; she will never know what has become of me and will think of me as a

"I would not want my mother to know of this." John Borich executed on 20 January 1919.

happy little boy. I wish I could see her once again" (*Salt Lake Tribune,* 16 Dec. 1919).

In his appearance before the Board of Pardons asking for commutation of his death sentence to life in prison, he argued that he could better pay for his crime and serve society if allowed to live. He presented himself as strong and healthy. His father had lived to the age of ninety-four. If allowed to live he could work and provide for Mrs. Adkins's children and be of use to society. The board declined.

His final will, written in the back of a diary, requested that most of his possessions be sent to his wife in Colorado and that his watch be given to her son from a previous marriage. He also ordered that what remained go to Mrs. Adkins's children.

One hundred fifty spectators were at the execution. His final statement was: "I am sorry I did this and I hope I will be forgiven. Good-by Warden; good-by Dave [Sheriff Adamson, Tooele County]; good-by prison; good-by everybody! God bless you all" (*Salt Lake Tribune,* 20 Dec. 1919).

* * *

Steve Maslich and Nick Oblizalo were the third pair to be executed in Utah. On 4 August 1919 the body of Marco Laus, a Colorado miner, was found in a ravine near the Utah State Prison in Sugarhouse by two trustees in charge of irrigating the prison farm. Laus had been killed the previous day. His throat was cut from ear to ear and there were twenty stab wounds in various parts of his body. Through inquiry among the Austrian community in Salt Lake, it was discovered that Laus had been seen with Maslich and Oblizalo. Maslich was arrested in Butte, Montana, and Oblizalo in Ely, Nevada.

Laus had recently arrived from Colorado. He was carrying $900 in gold coins and had asked among the Austrians living in Salt Lake City about depositing the money in a bank. When he found that he would receive paper currency instead of gold, he decided not to make the deposit. The

"A white handkerchief and an old world superstition." Steve Maslich executed on 20 January 1922.

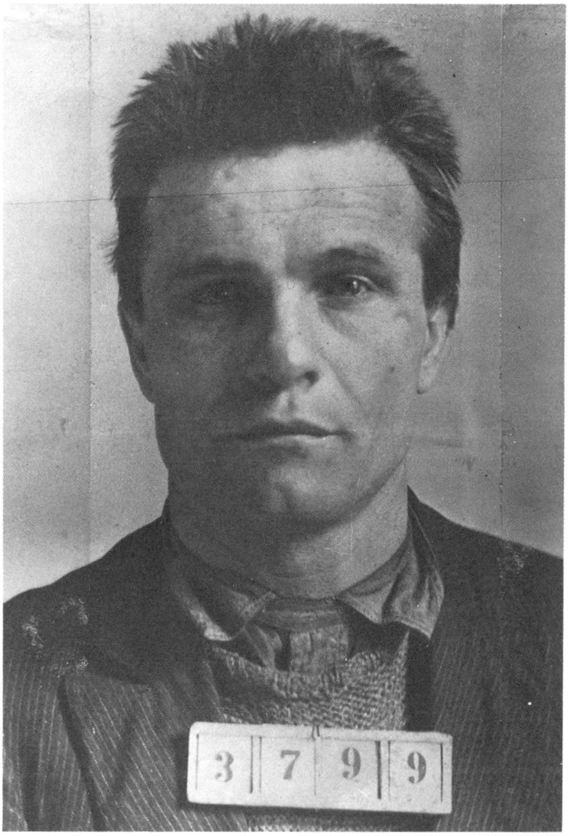

"Another Austrian." Nick Obizalo executed on 9 June 1922.

prosecution maintained a third person who was never identified lured Laus to the spot near the prison under the pretext of selling him a piece of property. Once there Maslich and Oblizalo stabbed him with pocketknives and robbed him.

After their arrests, Maslich and Oblizalo each blamed the other. Each was tried separately, and each was sentenced to die. Maslich's appeals process ran out first and he was sentenced to be executed by firing squad 20 January 1922. Those around him were surprised by his "attitude of stoic indifference" (*Deseret News,* 20 Jan. 1922). He apparently did not believe he would be executed. Up to the point where the black hood was placed over his head, he was laughing and joking. At one point he said, "Every day is better. You fellows are only fooling" (ibid.). A reporter for the *Tribune* (21 Jan. 1922) credited Maslich's cavalier attitude to Old World superstition. A white handkerchief was found next to Laus's body, and investigators learned that according to Old World tradition, a murderer could assure his or her last-minute reprieve by leaving behind a clean white handkerchief or other token of purity.

Oblizalo was executed five months later on 9 June 1922, also by firing squad.

* * *

On 15 April 1922 Deputy Sheriff Gordon Stuart, Joseph W. Irvine, and others went to the house of Irvine's brother-in-law, George H. Gardner, in Welby (near Sandy) with a warrant to repossess stock and equipment on the Gardner farm. They were first told by Gardner's common-law wife that he was not home. Later she changed her story and told the deputy to go up to the house. Irvine remained outside while Stuart and another officer approached the house and were invited in by Gardner. As they went ahead of him toward the parlor, Gardner produced a shotgun and fired twice. Stuart fell and his partner fled.

Gardner then jumped on a horse his wife had saddled

and took off after Irvine. When Gardner caught up with him, he shot him in the face and returned to the house. He and his wife stayed there until persuaded by a neighbor to surrender. Stuart died at the scene; Irvine passed away a few days later.

As a boy in Cache Valley, Gardner was called "cripple" by playmates because of a deformed leg, the result of scarlet fever. He was also considered "weakminded" and was continually taunted by other children. Not much else is known about Gardner. Prior to this crime there had been some problems, including a liquor raid on his farm house. Gardner was divorced and had a child from his previous marriage.

The day before the incident, Gardner's fourteen-year-old daughter accused him of sexually molesting her. "Gardner ruined me," she charged. Gardner's common-law wife, Martha Gerrons, had returned to the home that morning to confront him about the charge. The sheriff's deputies apparently interrupted them, and this no doubt helped to trigger the killings.

Both Gardner and his wife Martha were charged with murder. George was found guilty and sentenced to die by firing squad. Martha's trial ended in a hung jury after twenty-seven hours of deliberation. She was never retried. Gardner's attorneys argued before the State Board of Pardons that he was "subnormal" and "weakminded" and that his sentence ought to be commuted to life in prison. A petition containing hundreds of signatures supporting commutation was presented to the board. Among the signatures were those of four jurors who convicted Gardner.

All appeals failed. Gardner spent the night before his execution talking with the guards on death watch. They sat next to him on the cot and reported: "At no time . . . did he show any sign of breaking. He discussed his life, and . . . reiterated the declaration that his life had been a bed of thorns" (*Salt Lake Tribune,* 15 Jan. 1922). The next morning

"I have no apology to make for the killing of Irvine." George H. Gardner executed on 31 August 1923.

he ordered milk and oatmeal for his last meal: "As the death march started, prisoners in the cell house called goodbye and made the prison ghastly with their eerie shrieks . . . but he [Gardner] kept walking as steadily and deliberately as his shriveled leg would permit. There were no heroics. He acted natural" (ibid.).

Gardner was executed by firing squad at 6:30 a.m. on 31 August 1923. His last statement was, "The killing of Gordon Stuart was accidental, but I have no apology to make for the killing of Irvine" (*Salt Lake Telegram,* 31 Aug. 1923). Each member of the firing squad was paid $40. The total execution cost was $200 (*Ogden Standard Examiner,* 31 Aug. 1923). Gardner was buried in his hometown, Mendon, Utah.

Among those present at the execution was one who claimed to have been present at every execution since statehood. The *Salt Lake Telegram* reported on 31 August 1923 that this spectator "declared that Gardner displayed the least emotion of any of the long list who have been compelled to pay the price society demands for murder."

* * *

On 9 January 1922 firemen discovered the body of Myretta Woods at the Pauline Apartments, Third East and First South. She had been bound and gagged, hit in the face with a blunt object, strangled, and her body set on fire. Her husband, Omer R. Woods, told the firemen that two men had entered the apartment while Mrs. Woods and he were having lunch. They robbed and beat him, then tied him up and locked him in the closet. Suspicion focused on Woods when inconsistencies were found in his story, and he was arrested for the murder of his wife.

Myretta Woods was an invalid, suffering from tuberculosis. She was described as "a frail, delicate woman of quiet and friendly disposition and to have had few acquaintances in the city" (*Salt Lake Tribune,* 10 Jan. 1922). Her husband was employed by the U.S. Revenue Service as an estate tax inspector. He was a former attorney, had served

"A former attorney, judge, and school teacher." Omer R. Woods executed on 18 January 1924.

as a probate judge in Idaho City in Boise County, and had been a school teacher. The Woods had a nineteen-year-old daughter, Tee Lee Woods, a student at the University of Utah.

On 17 January 1924 the Salt Lake County Commission (under whose jurisdiction the execution was to be conducted) appropriated $350 to cover the expense of Woods's execution. Governor Mabey refused to grant a commutation: "Those who have urged commutation of the death sentence are not familiar with the facts of the case as presented to me and to other members of the pardons board. They plead for mercy in the name of humanity, but do not take into consideration the inhumanity of the murder. The pleas are the result of maudlin sympathy. There is nothing to be done but to carry out the death sentence" (*Salt Lake Tribune,* 18 Jan. 1924).

The morning of his execution, 18 January 1924, Woods ordered a meal of southern fried chicken, sweet potatoes, and coffee. As he approached the firing squad, he was smoking a black cigar. He called out from his chair near the south wall of the prison in Sugarhouse, "The last thing that I do is send a kiss to my mother, sister, to my daughter, and to my daughter again." His last words proclaimed his innocence: "I believe—and it is my dying statement—that [A. C.] Vadney [of Council, Idaho] was the smaller of the two robbers. I am as innocent today as I was the day my mother gave me birth. I am prepared to meet my maker in peace" (*Ogden Standard Examiner,* 18 Jan. 1924). Within seconds he was dead. He was buried at Mt. Olivet Cemetery in Salt Lake. His mother in Tennessee was never told of the execution.

* * *

On 27 November 1922 police sergeant Nephi P. Pierce and patrolman G. P. Watson were walking their beat along Fifth South and Main Street in Salt Lake City, looking for two men who had been involved in several robberies in the area. Seeing two men—Henry C. Hett and Arthur Hayes—Sergeant Pierce called for them to stop. Hett pulled a revolver and ordered the officers to raise their hands. Pierce began to back away and was shot by Hett. Hayes fled, but Hett ordered Patrolman Watson into a vacant lot where he pistol-whipped him and then escaped. Pierce, who had been with the police force twelve years, died four months later in March 1923. Hett and Hayes were arrested the next day. At their trial, both were found guilty of first degree murder—Hett was sentenced to death, Hayes was given a life sentence after the jury returned a recommendation for mercy.

The killing of Nephi Pierce ended a twelve-day crime spree by Hett and Hayes in two states, Colorado and Utah. After their arrest both men were taken to the hospital bedside of Pierce, who positively identified the two men as his assailants. The bullet had severed his spine and left him paralyzed from the waist down. He requested that his wife not be immediately told because she was "afflicted with a nervous disorder." In fact, the *Salt Lake Telegram* reported on 20 February 1925 that Mrs. Pierce died a short while after her husband's death, "the tragedy, it is believed, having hastened her death."

Hett had lost both parents when he was young. He and Hayes had been on their own as youths and had learned survival "on the road." Since Hayes did not do the actual shooting and fled when the shots were fired, he was sentenced to life in prison. His case was eventually reversed by the state supreme court and a retrial was ordered. After his new trial, he was sentenced to prison for attempted robbery. He was paroled on 16 October 1926 after serving three years, ten months, and four days.

Hett was executed by firing squad 20 February 1925. Prior to his execution he left a final letter for the press: "Ere this reaches your readers my spirit will be wafted before my Maker and my body consigned to the grave. I surrender my life conscious of my sin and the penalty it imposes, also regretful and repentant for the crime. I have naught to give

"The last few hours have been the happiest in my life." Henry C. Hett executed on 20 February 1925.

towards restitution save my sorrow and my life—would that I had more" (*Salt Lake Telegram,* 20 Feb. 1925). After commenting on his trial and expressing his appreciation to those who had helped him, he concluded: "In closing, a word to the boys in this prison. I shall not feel that I have died in vain if my passing will show to you that there is only one road that leads to happiness, and that is the straight and narrow path of honesty, virtue and truth. Please do not treat this as only the dying admonition of a fellow convict. Its observance by you will mean to me that my sacrifice may prove your salvation" (ibid.).

Just before leaving his cell for the "death march," Hett commented to the press, "I might add the last few hours have been the happiest in my life. I say this with no spirit of braggadocio. I say it sincerely" (*Salt Lake Telegram,* 20 Feb. 1925). As he sat in the chair awaiting the order to fire, he kept repeating over and over, "I'm sorry, I'm sorry, I'm sorry" (ibid.).

* * *

On 15 March 1923 June St. Clair of Park City, Utah, was heard screaming by one of her neighbors. The neighbor ran over but could not enter the locked door. He found an ax in a shed, broke the front window, and entered the cabin. He found St. Clair dying of a stab wound to the heart. Pedro Cano was arrested by police after they followed a trail of blood from St. Clair's cabin to Cano's home. It was believed he had cut his hand on a broken rear window as he escaped.

Cano, a Mexican national, had been in Park City about two weeks. He was an unemployed miner and claimed that he had exchanged a greeting with the "American lady" as he was cleaning snow off the sidewalk. He was living with a woman at the time named Alemeda, and she became jealous. He denied that he and St. Clair were romantically involved, but he and Alemeda quarrelled about her. Cano felt things had calmed down later that afternoon. He left for a time and returned to find St. Clair and Alemeda arguing.

The next day he returned home from playing pool to find Alemeda dressed in men's clothing. She sprang at him with a knife, cutting his hand and face. He locked himself in the kitchen, and, according to the court transcript, she yelled if she "could not fix me she would go over and kill the American woman." She then left wearing his hat and coat. The next thing he knew, the police were at his door to arrest him.

Since he spoke no English, Cano was given an interpreter for the trial. According to Cano, this interpreter was Alemeda's friend and tried to convince Cano "not to give Refugia Alemeda away." He told Cano that "if she was my sweetheart it was not manly on my part to give her away." Cano said that the interpreter knew she was guilty and offered him $1,000 not to expose her. Cano claimed he told the interpreter he wanted to tell the truth, but the interpreter did not translate what Cano said. Instead he protected Alemeda throughout the investigation and trial.

Cano was found guilty and sentenced to die by firing squad. While on death row, he kept himself busy making beaded purses which the warden sold to help support Cano's mother. He was executed 15 May 1925, maintaining his innocence to the end. In a prepared statement, Cano stated: "Is it not better to die and start a new life with an opportunity to accomplish something than to be imprisoned for life behind the cold gray bars and accomplish nothing?" (*Salt Lake Tribune,* 16 May 1925). His last words were, "I am innocent. Seek the woman [Refugia Alemeda], and take care of my mother" (*Ogden Standard Examiner,* 17 May 1925).

The Salt Lake City cemetery refused burial for Cano. Carlos Ariza, Mexican Consul in Salt Lake City, pointed out that previously executed men (Hett, Woods, and Gardner) were buried in city cemeteries. He threatened court action unless either a permit was issued permitting the burial of Cano or the bodies of the others were disinterred and buried

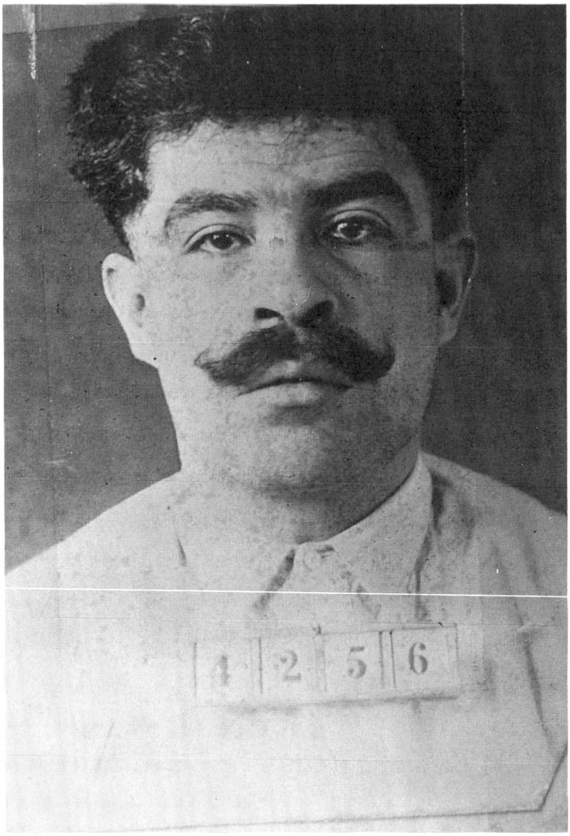

"I am innocent. Seek the woman." Pedro Cano executed on 15 May 1925.

outside the city limits: "It is an outrage on decency and if we are not permitted to give Cano decent burial the world shall know of it. If necessary we shall go into court and inquire into the constitutionality of a law that apparently seeks to pursue a man for an alleged offense even after he has, perhaps unjustly, paid the supreme penalty for his alleged crime" (*Ogden Standard Examiner,* 16 Jan. 1926).

On 19 May 1925 the city commission amended the ordinance, and Cano was allowed burial. Only one commission member opposed the change.

* * *

On 12 October 1923 the body of Salt Lake police officer David H. Crowther was found on the bank of the Jordan River near North Temple. He had been shot once in the back of the head. It was believed he had been shot by transients, since he had spent a great deal of time in that area running them out of town. His car was missing and was later identified near San Bernardino, California, where three men—Ralph Seyboldt (alias Ralph Sanders), Joseph Eli Marenger (alias Fred Dupont), and Noel E. White (alias George F. Williams)—were arrested and extradited. Marenger and White pled guilty to second degree murder and were given twenty-year sentences. Seyboldt was found guilty of first degree murder and sentenced to death by firing squad.

Seyboldt's conviction was based on the testimony of his companions, who said he had killed Crowther, shooting him in the head in order to steal his vehicle. Seyboldt later confessed. The three of them had arrived in Salt Lake City from Rawlins, Wyoming. A few days later Crowther picked them up and took them for a ride. While riding, Seyboldt killed the officer, hid his body in the brush, and the three of them headed for California. It took the jury fifteen minutes to find Seyboldt guilty—a record. There was no recommendation for mercy.

During the next two years, Seyboldt was given several stays and seven hearings before the Board of Pardons. At the time

"A cop killer." Ralph Seyboldt executed on 15 January 1926.

of his execution, the press made an issue of the length of time that had elapsed between his crime and execution. The *Salt Lake Tribune* marked it as "two years, three months and three days after the commission of the crime, October 12, 1923."

Just prior to Seyboldt's execution, his father and several others from his hometown of Defiance, Ohio, appealed to the governor and to President Coolidge for clemency. His estranged wife, Rilla Seyboldt, avoided reporters. Seyboldt died by firing squad at 8:01 a.m., 15 January 1926.

Marenger was paroled on 1 July 1930 to his mother and sister in California. White, who was sixteen at the time of the killing, was paroled on 19 May 1934.

* * *

On 11 January 1924 at about 5:00 p.m. Edward McGowan entered the home of Bob Blevins in Helper, Utah. He was on friendly terms with the family and had visited there often. Blevins's wife Susie was home. She claimed McGowan had been drinking and began to force himself on her. Her adopted daughter Eva returned home and was also forced into the back bedroom. Bob Blevins then returned home and was forced at gunpoint into the bedroom, where he was shot in the abdomen while arguing with McGowan.

At this point a second adopted daughter, thirteen-year-old Mary, returned home. McGowan forced the three women to submit to sexual acts with him throughout the night until 5:00 the next morning when he left. Medical aid was immediately sought for Blevins, but he died around noon, 12 January. McGowan was captured near Soldier Summit that afternoon.

McGowan was the first black man executed in Utah. The victim and his family were all black as well. McGowan claimed Mrs. Blevins had made "improper advances" toward him. He refused her advances and she threatened him with a pistol. The two of them scuffled with the pistol, and it went off just as Blevins entered the room. He tried to en-

"He didn't die with his boots on." Edward McGowan executed on 5 February 1926.

courage Mrs. Blevins to get help but she refused, preferring to treat him herself until morning.

McGowan was found guilty and sentenced to die by firing squad. In a final statement, he wrote:

> Ere this will have been handed to and read by you, my soul will have been wafted before its Maker. My last wish and desire on this earth will be realized when I am able to have published my closing words in the form of advice to the youth of the nation. To you I say obey your parents, seek the advice of your elders, and live an honest and clean life with thoughts of bright and cleaner things, at all times seek the finer things in life, and by all means obey the teachings of God and be able through these teachings to receive ultimate celestial glory (*Salt Lake Telegram,* 5 Feb. 1926).

As McGowan was led to the place of execution, he wore a pair of old rubber shoes. His last request was granted—that he not die with his "boots on." As he raised his hand to wave farewell, the rifles fired; sixty-two seconds later McGowan was dead. He was buried in the prison cemetery. He had requested that "he receive a decent burial and that his body not be sent to some institution to be cut up" (*Salt Lake Telegram,* 5 Feb. 1926). The inmates had raised money to help with burial costs should it be needed.

5.

HARDENED CRIMINALS

Ten years elapsed from the time of Edward McGowan's execution in 1926 to Delbert Green's. Calvin Coolidge had been succeeded by Franklin D. Roosevelt as president of the United States; George H. Dern had been replaced by Henry H. Blood as governor of Utah, while Heber J. Grant remained president of the LDS church. Utah's population had grown from 449,000 to 550,000.

In 1926 Utah reported the second highest divorce rate in the country and the third highest automobile death rate. The governor of Texas that year granted clemency to 1,315 people, including 821 pardons. Ten years later Utah's governor was considering a new site for the old Sugarhouse prison, and in Ogden a triple slayer had just been arrested for using a pick-axe handle to kill the parents and grandmother of his estranged wife. George Mortenson was arrested in Los Angeles five days before the execution of Delbert Green who killed his uncle, mother-in-law, and wife. Mortenson plead guilty, claiming he just "went crazy." Green, however, despite his protests of insanity, would be executed on 10 July 1936.

* * *

Returning home from the Ogden junk yard where he worked, Delbert Green found that his wife had taken their baby daughter and left him. Green believed his wife had been unfaithful and that her mother and stepfather (actually Green's uncle) had interfered in their marriage.

Green's mother-in-law and stepfather/uncle lived with Green's grandmother in Layton. Green went there after work and found his wife. After talking with her he left for Ogden. Later that night he returned to Layton. Claiming that he feared his uncle was going to shoot him, Green shot the uncle. The mother-in-law, his wife, and the baby were sleeping together in a bed in the same room. Hearing the shots, they sat up and Green shot them, one of them falling over and covering the baby with her body. According to Green, he then walked outside and tried to shoot himself, but the gun jammed. He next found his uncle's shotgun, and planned to kill himself but could find no shells. Finally he returned home and went to bed. He was found the next morning with the covers pulled over his head.

Green claimed his family had a history of insanity. His father was an inmate of an asylum when he died; an aunt had been sent to an asylum; his grandfather had committed suicide. It was also testified that Green had the mentality of a nine- or ten-year-old. Previously Green had served time in the Utah state prison for attempted murder.

Prior to Green's execution, 282 inmates at the prison signed a petition:

> We respectfully ask, in view of the circumstances of his case which you know so well, that you commute his sentence to life imprisonment. To us, Delbert Green is a friend. We submit that we are unqualified to pass upon his mental condition as others have and base our conclusions wholly upon association and contact with him over a period of years. Men of science have passed upon that and found him to have the mind of a ten year old child. Unqualified judges though we are, we too think

Delbert Green to be mentally deficient. We respectfully submit that you would not permit a ten year old child to die before a rifle blast fired by the State of Utah and so we humbly ask that you do not permit the same fate to befall a man whose mental condition places him in the same category of a child.[1]

Green's mother appealed to the governor:

> Mr. Blood, I am the mother of 8 children, 4 boys and 4 girls. Delbert's two sisters are married and have children. I have 5 by another marriage, the oldest a boy of 18 years. I have been a widow for seven years. I also have Delbert[s] baby, she is 5 years old now. I have been sick for 2 years and haven't been able to work, so if you can please lift some of this load from my back by giving life imprisonment instead of death. Please do this much for us.[2]

In another letter to Governor Blood, Green appealed for his own life:

> All I ask is that you give me a fair and impartial decision. Again, I ask you to read closely the record of my unhappy marriage. I loved my wife with a great love, and I still love and cherish her memory. But she was unfaithful to me. This caused another great worry to me. I tried to stop it in the only way I could think of, but it turned out to be another tragedy which I could not help. I thought I could frighten the fellow that she was out with, by displaying a gun, but he became hysterical and grabbed the weapon, and during our scuffle for its possession it discharged and a bullet struck him. Yet this did not destroy my love for my wife. She asked me to plead guilty to the charge to protect her from letting her

"She was unfaithful to me." Delbert Green executed on 10 July 1936.

Delbert Green's mother-in-law, Mrs. James Green, and his wife, Gladys Green—both victims of his crime. Courtesy Lorraine Green, daughter of Delbert Green.

> friends know about her unfaithfulness to me. I loved her and pleaded guilty to the charge. You would have done the same, if one of your loved ones had asked you to do it. And especially the one you loved more than anything else in this world.

He concluded his letter:

> My little daughter was down here to visit me yesterday, and these are the words that came from her little lips. "Daddy, I want to take you home with me." You will never be able to understand the heartache that sentence caused me. Surely you do not want to take a little girl's daddy from her, and place a greater burden upon the shoulders of a dear old mother, who's staggering already under a heavy load. All I ask is that you give this letter your serious consideration. Free from politics and prejudice and what ever your decision is, I will take like a man (*Salt Lake Tribune,* 10 July 1936).

Green was executed at the old prison at Sugarhouse on 10 July 1936. His execution was witnessed by over seventy-five people, while "throngs" waited outside along Twenty-First South in Salt Lake City to hear the five .30-.30's. Mayor Harman W. Peery of Ogden attended the execution. He had been at the Ute Stampede in Nephi and told the *Salt Lake Tribune,* 11 July 1936, "I just decided to drop in here on my way home."

Green's mother gave him a card the night before the execution. On the front it read, "He is just away," and inside contained a verse by James Whitcomb Riley. The next morning Green was escorted from the prison chapel where he had spent the night with the Catholic prison chaplain, a member of the Granite School District, and four of his relatives. As he entered the open air, a black hood was placed over his face, and he was guided to the chair in which he would die. His only words were, "My God! Have mercy on me." The chair was along the wall at the south side of the prison. Thirty feet away the five rifles fired, and a small black and silver crucifix fell from Green's hands.

Lorraine Green was seven years old at the time of her father's execution. She recalled her "father was a very loving and devoted person. He gave my mother everything in the world to make her happy, but she was unfaithful. And her mother was always interfering. My Dad was very easy going and patient. My Dad finally had it. He got the gun. I was only four months old" (*Ogden Standard Examiner,* 17 Jan. 1977). Forty-one years later, at the time of Gary Gilmore's execution,Green, still living in Ogden, reminisced: "I remember my father from the time I was three. He was all I had. [My grandmother] raised me. She took me every Sunday to see my dad until the time they executed him" (ibid.).

* * *

On 9 May 1938 at approximately 9:00 p.m., fifty-two-year-old Oliver Meredith, Jr., a real estate and leather goods businessman, was found shot and bleeding in his parked automobile in front of the Madsen Apartments (169 South Fifth East). He died a few minutes later after being carried into the apartment where he lived with his wife. About three months later, John W. Deering was arrested in Detroit, Michigan, on suspicion of robbery. He told Detroit police he was wanted in Salt Lake City for murder and "I want to go back there and die" (*Salt Lake Tribune,* 31 Oct. 1938).

Deering had been committed to a reformatory at the age of thirteen as a neglected child. He was released at age eighteen and began a life of crime that took him through San Quentin, the Merchant Marines, and Folsom prison. He spent no more than three years outside of prison or reformatory walls from the age of thirteen. He was found guilty of first degree murder in Salt Lake City and at the time of sentencing amazed the judge who later wrote:

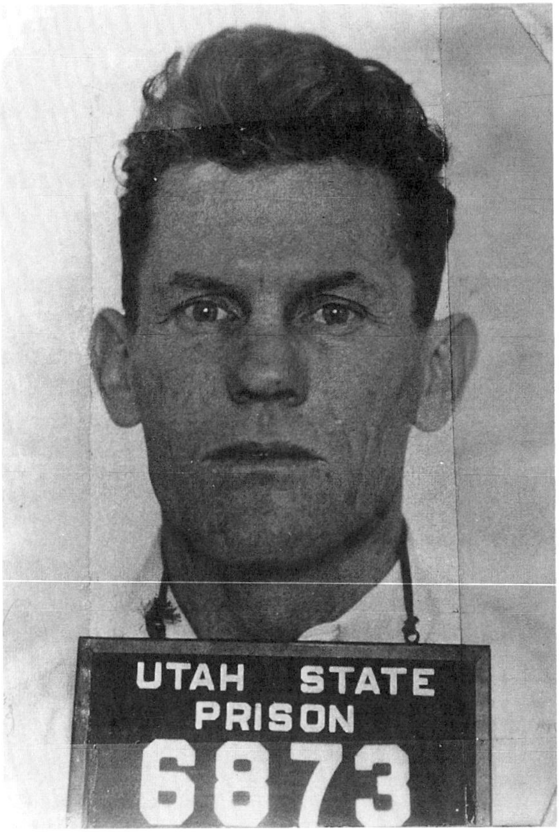

"Telltale Heart." John W. Deering executed on 31 October 1938.

> He was duly arraigned before me on a charge of first degree murder. In the first instance he refused counsel, although the Court offered to provide him with counsel, and he assumed the most extraordinary attitude to which my attention has been called in a criminal case. He stated to the Court that he stood upon his constitutional right to enter a plea of guilty, and immediately to face the firing squad.[3]

Deering agreed to allow the prison physician to monitor his heartbeat on an electrocardiogram during the execution. At the time of his execution, Deering's heartbeat went from seventy-two beats per minute to one hundred eighty when he was strapped in the chair. His heart stopped beating 15.6 seconds after the bullets entered his body. As a last wish he had willed his eyes to an optics specialist in California and his body to the University of Utah, stating that at last he would get some "high class education."[4]

* * *

On 20 March 1941 Donald Lawton Condit drove through a red light, was chased by law enforcement officers, ran into a tree at University Street and Seventh South, and was arrested. He was driving a car belonging to a grocery salesman, Harold Arthur Thorne, whose wife expressed surprise that the car was in Salt Lake City. Her husband had been on the road and last heard from in Las Vegas. After several hours of questioning, Condit admitted that he had been hitchhiking and that Thorne had picked him up. Thorne's body was found covered with brush along the side of the highway about ten miles west of Cedar City. He had been hit on the head with a rock.

At the age of seven, Condit's family had been poisoned by eating spoiled olives while living in southern California. His mother died immediately of ptomaine poisoning; his only brother, age seventeen, died three days later—leaving Donald, his father, and his five year-old sister. He and his

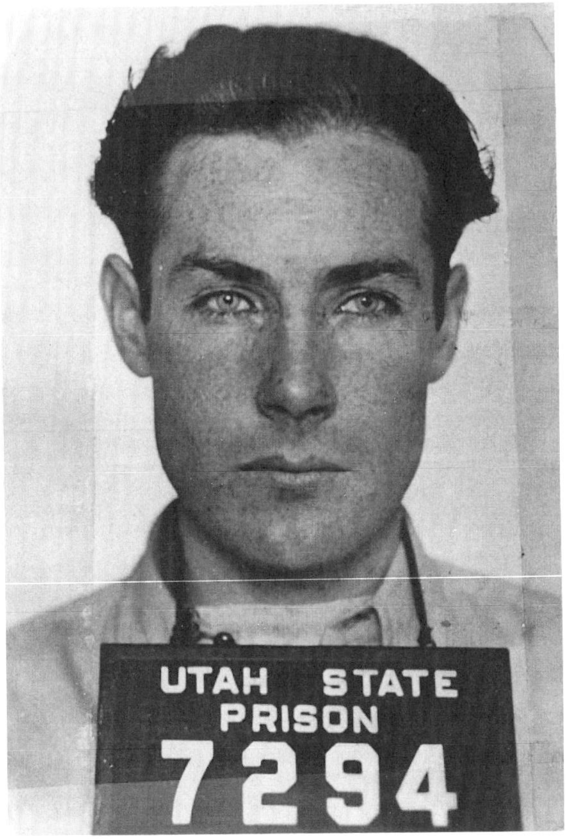

"Poisoned olives cost him his happy family." Donald Condit executed on 30 July 1942.

sister went to live with a wealthy grand-uncle and grand-aunt and began attending a series of exclusive boarding schools. His sister went on to become a teacher at Columbia University, but Donald went from military schools to private schools to reform schools to prisons. One analyst suggested that Condit "has not been much with his father since [the age of seven and], getting into trouble, he seemed to have learned quite young, would bring his father to him."[5]

After his release from San Quentin in 1940, Condit met and married his wife Betty but shortly thereafter lost his job because his employer did not like his parole officer checking on him during work hours. With no job or prospects, Condit became despondent: "Bucking the same barrier several times everyday for over two weeks became terribly discouraging, and it began to most hurtfully show on my lovely bride, Betty. I guess I then began despondently thinking Betty would be better off if I wasn't in her life."[6]

After considering suicide, he decided to leave California and find employment elsewhere. He phoned his wife saying he would not be home that night and took a bus to San Bernardino, where he stole a car and drove to Las Vegas. From there he hitched a ride with Thorne. At this point, Condit claims he showed his gun to Thorne with the intent of selling it to him. Thorne misunderstood his intentions, grabbed for the gun, and was accidentally shot in the struggle. However, the prosecution maintained Condit intended to rob Thorne from the beginning.

Condit died by firing squad on 30 July 1942. One half hour before his death, he was given morphine as a sedative. When asked if he had any final statement he said, "No I guess not, I can't see any use of all this though" (*Deseret News,* 30 July 1942).

* * *

On 11 February 1941, around closing time at 6:30 p.m., a robbery was taking place at the Safeway Store on 24th and Grant in Ogden. Robert Walter Avery had left his wife sitting outside in the car. He entered the store and informed the clerks, "This is a stick-up." The manager, R. K. Yeates, was on the phone with his wife and had just enough time to tell her to call the police before being ordered to hang up. Mrs. Yeates called the police and told them there was "trouble" at the store. Not knowing what to expect, Officer Hoyt L. Gates hurried over and entered through the door. According to witnesses, Avery began to shoot, hitting Gates, who was barely able to return fire before crawling back outside. He died a few minutes later. The Averys escaped with $150.

Avery was the first man to be sentenced to death from Weber County (Delbert Green, although from Weber County, committed his crime in Davis County). He started stealing at the age of sixteen and eventually spent time in Leavenworth and in the Nevada state prison. He came to Salt Lake City from San Francisco with his wife, Roverda Avery, and together were later suspected in other robberies, including one at the Ambassador Hotel where they were staying.

On 10 February 1941, Avery stood outside the Safeway store in Ogden, observing closing hours and other details he would need to know in preparation for the robbery. The next day his wife parked on Washington Avenue between 23rd and 24th streets to await his return. After the ill-fated robbery, she too was arrested but later released.

The day before his execution, Avery's autobiography was released. In it he wrote:

> Death to me is simply the cashing in of a stack of chips all of us receive at birth and while I have lost heavily in the game of life, I intend to face the cashier as a good loser. I have played my cards as I found them.... But when I reached the place where all my marked cards were recognized . . . the game was practically over for me. This time I've been called and I'm going to shove in the rest of my chips with a smile (*Ogden Standard Examiner,* 4 Feb. 1943).

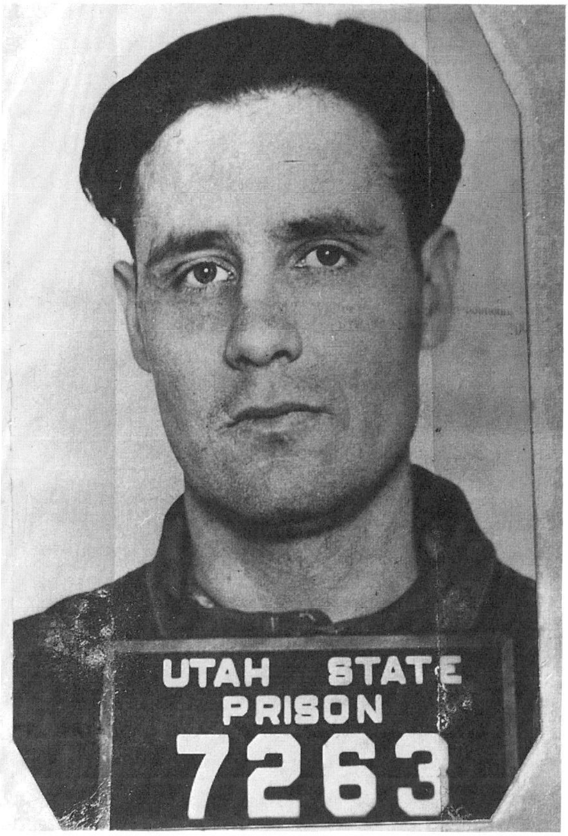

"Death is simply the cashing in of a stack of chips and I intend to face the cashier as a good loser." Robert Walter Avery executed on 5 February 1943.

His last meal was a cheese sandwich and a can of grapefruit juice. As he was seated in the chair before the firing squad, two messages could be seen—apparently written by inmates with access to the storage area where the execution equipment was kept. Just behind the chair was written, "The Last Mile," and at the side was "Crime Never Pays."[7]

* * *

On the night of 23 July 1943, at about 11:30, Judge Lewis V. Trueman and his wife were in their Ogden home at 1543 Twenty-seventh street when a shotgun blast was fired through their kitchen window. Trueman turned on the light in the hallway and together with his wife went to the window of their bedroom to see what was going on. As they did, another shot was fired, striking the judge in the head and neck and killing him.

Austin Cox, who fired the shots, next went to the police station and entered with shotgun in hand. Chambering another round, he announced, "I will kill every son of a bitch in here." After firing a wild shot, he was subdued and arrested.

Cox had apparently heard his ex-wife was staying at 2240 Lincoln Avenue and had gone there looking for her. They had recently divorced after being married only seven weeks. Once there he killed four and wounded two people before moving on to Trueman's home and then to the police station. Trueman had presided over the Coxes' divorce proceedings. Wanda Mae Carter described her ex-husband as "being of a mean and jealous disposition." She had at one time filed a battery complaint against him, claiming he beat her and threatened to cut out her tongue. He in turn accused her of giving him a venereal disease and of sleeping with other men. Those who had worked with Cox described him as "a person who continuously had fancied grievances" and who felt himself picked on (*Ogden Standard Examiner,* 24 July 1943).

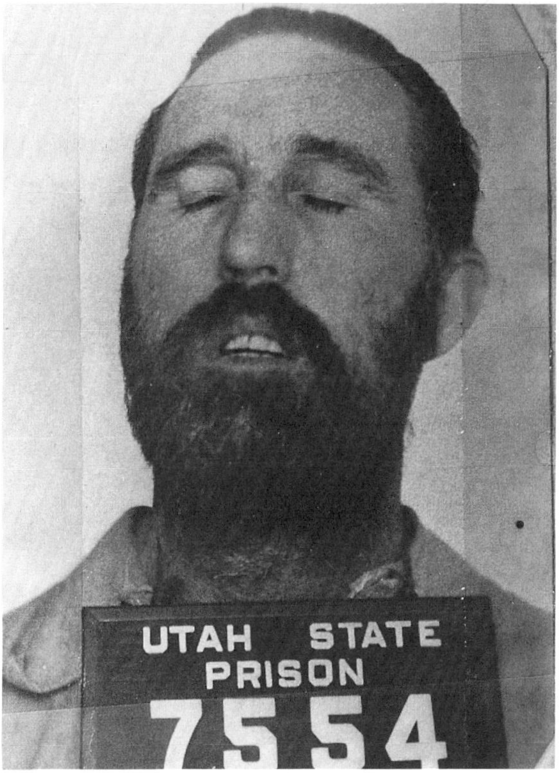

"Being of a mean and jealous disposition." Austin Cox, Jr., executed on 19 June 1944.

Cox had not appeared at divorce court because he felt he was being persecuted and his "enemies" would prevail against him. He had told others that he would get the judge, the sheriff, two of the deputies, and his wife—that he would "catch the whole bunch together and get them all." At his trial his wife testified she told him he should not kill. He responded "that he had worked for seven years around the State Mental Hospital of Arizona and that he could 'beat a murder rap' because he had been around those 'nuts' there enough to feign insanity."[8] Cox's insanity defense was not successful. He was found guilty of first degree murder without recommendation for leniency and was sentenced to die. After a last meal of strawberries and cream, he was executed by firing squad at 6:00 a.m. on 19 June 1944. The *Salt Lake Tribune* (9 July 1944) reported that his execution cost $653.

* * *

James Joseph Roedl and LeRoy Edward Ritchie were hitch-hiking to Idaho on 12 October 1942. Around Denver, Colorado, they were picked up by Abigail Agnes Williams, a California school teacher and follower of Aimee Semple McPhearson, founder of the International Church of the Foursquare Gospel. Williams wanted someone to share gas costs. In the vicinity of Ft. Duchesne, along Highway 40, Roedl struck her on the head with a hammer as she lay asleep in the back seat of her car. They dumped her body by the side of the road along with her dog and luggage and left with the car. Both Roedl and Ritchie were arrested in Washington.

Roedl and Ritchie were first tried and convicted in the U.S. District Court, since the killing occurred on an Indian Reservation. However, the conviction was later dismissed because "non-Indian offenses occurring on an Indian Reservation do not come under federal law." Retried in Vernal, Utah, both were found guilty—Roedl sentenced to death and Ritchie, because of the jury's recommendation for leniency, to life in prison.

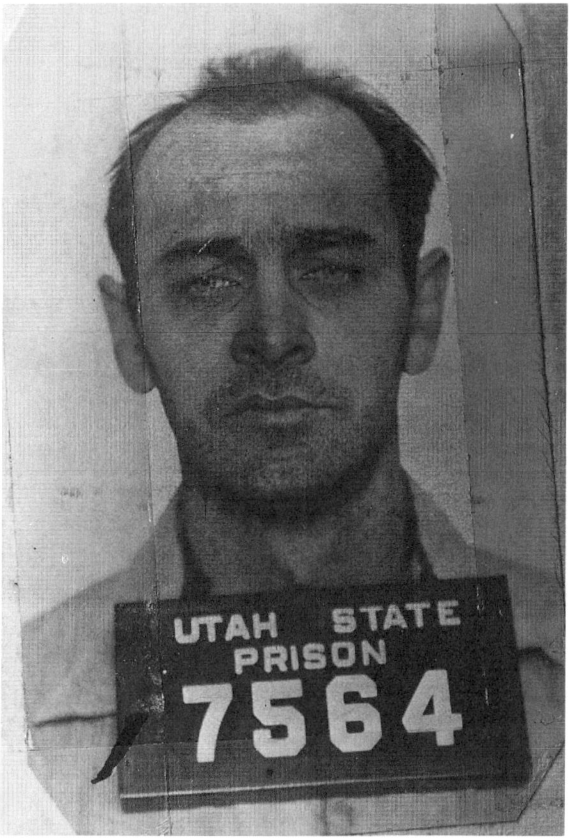

"I too should be given a life sentence." James Joseph Roedl executed on 13 July 1945.

In a letter to the Board of Pardons dated 14 June 1945, Roedl protested:

> As you men know in the eyes of the law my partner in this crime is as equally guilty as I am. He is to serve a life sentence. In justice, I too should be given a life sentence. If we are both guilty in the eyes of the law then we both should be given the same sentence. I have suffered from epilepsy and have been in an insane asylum. My co-partner is a perfect physical young man and is in full possession of his mental faculties. Yet he is to serve a life sentence for being guilty of the murder while for the same crime, my part calls for execution.[9]

Roedl was executed 13 July 1945 at the Utah State Prison in Sugarhouse, the last man to be executed there. He enjoyed a final meal with his father, who had come from Oklahoma. They had T-bone steaks, potatoes, asparagus tips, coffee, and pie. Ritchie eventually died of tuberculosis in an Ogden sanitarium—still under the jurisdiction of the Utah State Prison.

* * *

AWOL from the army, Eliseo Mares was traveling toward Wyoming in a stolen car. The car developed engine trouble near Sinclair, Wyoming. Mares joined up with another traveler, Jack Derwood Stallings of San Jose, California, who was also having car trouble. Using Mares's money, they continued their trip in Stallings's car. Stallings arranged to have his girlfriend wire some money to Ogden, Utah, where they would pick it up. On the way toward Weber Canyon, they continued to have car trouble and, as they worked on it, they also began drinking heavily.

Mares's story was that they were attacked by "cowboys" when they stopped at a tavern in Echo Canyon just before the Utah border. When he came to, Stallings was driving the car "with a wild look in his eyes" and his left eye was partly out of the socket:

> [Coming down Weber Canyon after leaving Echo Junction] I started hollering for help as the car careened down the canyon road. I then kicked Jack's foot off the accelerator in an effort to slow down the speed of the car. . . . When it came to a turn, I grabbed the steering wheel and turned it off the road where it came to a stop against a bank about a mile and a quarter west of the town of Echo. Jack had a wild look on his face. I jumped into the back seat. Jack then slid out from under the wheel and started toward me with a tire iron in his hand and muttering that he would kill me.[10]

Mares said he subdued Stallings, turned the car around, and headed toward Salt Lake City for help. When he got near Hoytsville, he noticed Stallings had quit breathing so he dumped the body out near a canal and continued down Parley's Canyon. The prosecution charged that Mares intended to steal the car and consciously killed Stallings. He disposed of Stallings's possessions to escape being caught.

Mares was born in Crowley, Colorado. His father served as night marshal and deputy sheriff. At the time of his crime, he was eighteen years old. He had gone AWOL to be with his wife and new baby. His father advised him to return to his post. He was on his way back when he stole the car.

Mares claimed self-defense to the end. However, the jury did not believe his story, and he met death by firing squad on 10 September 1951. His was the first execution conducted in the new prison at Point of the Mountain. The prison itself was not completed, but the execution was arranged in the maximum security area. A reporter later described the execution, using the name "Lee" (probably a shortened form of Eliseo):

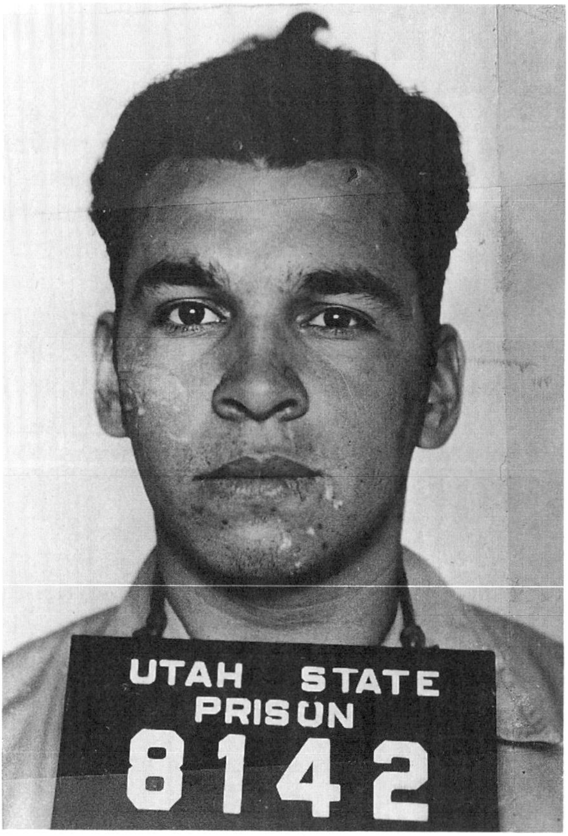

"The five marksmen missed the target twice." Eliseo Mares executed on 10 September 1951.

> He died silently—and horribly. The five [marksmen]—all volunteers—missed the target twice from their slit in a canvas curtain hiding their identity. It struck me then, and it does now, that it was incredible that rifles on a rest about 15 feet away from a condemned man could strike him in the stomach and hip. But it happened. Although no one will know absolutely whether the shots blotted out consciousness earlier, it was several minutes before Lee was pronounced dead (*Salt Lake Tribune,* 18 July 1976).

* * *

On 20 July 1949 Shirley Gretzinger kissed her mother goodbye and left for a babysitting job. She had not planned on going out that evening, but a friend was sick and had referred the caller to Shirley. Shirley's mother was concerned because she did not know who Shirley would be sitting for.

Instead of picking her up, the caller had arranged to meet Shirley at the corner of 34th and Washington in Ogden. She was last seen walking with a "short, dark-haired handsome man." Her body was found the next morning in Riverdale, but another month passed before Ray Dempsey Gardner, an itinerant cherry picker, was arrested and charged with the murder.

Gardner had spent time in several institutions, including the Indiana Boy's School, Montana State Prison, and the Wyoming State Prison. His father had died in a shoot-out with police, and his mother later went to jail. He was born and raised in an orphanage in Columbus, Ohio, and had been in trouble most of his life, accumulating over 300 offenses, including two homicides.

His execution took place on the grounds of the prison at Point of the Mountain. An old wooden chair was set on a raised, straw-covered platform. His last words were, "I'm ready to go. No one will miss me. My life has been worthless."[11] Apparently he was right. When the warden of the

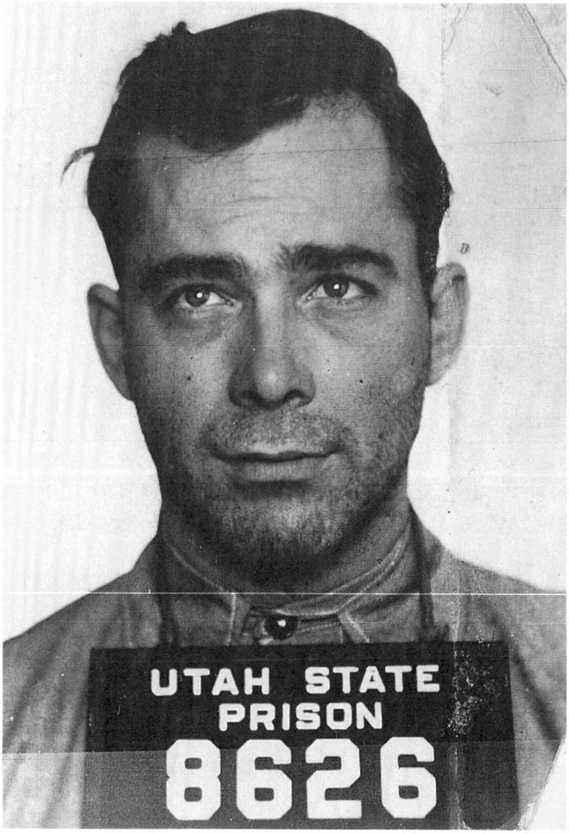

"No one will miss me." Ray Dempsey Gardner executed on 29 July 1951.

prison wrote his grandmother, his nearest living relative, she responded: "In referring to your letter . . . in regard to Ray Gardner's body being shipped to Ohio. I am not able to have him sent here . . . his mother is dead. We knew nothing about him for eight years until we read of him committing the crime. . . . I have no further responsibility of care. Use the body as the law directs for medical science."[12]

* * *

On 23 May 1951 Don Jesse Neal and his "girl friend," Wilma L. (Buster) Tulley, drove a 1951 DeSoto into downtown Salt Lake City, parked it near Third South and Main Street, and went shopping. In the meantime police had identified the car as stolen. When Neal and Tulley returned, Neal was placed under arrest and his hands cuffed behind his back.

Officer Owen T. Farley climbed into the front seat of the DeSoto, with Neal beside him and Tulley on the right. According to witnesses, the car went a few feet and then swerved into the rear of a parked car. Tulley ran out the right door, and Farley fell out the same door, calling he was shot and needed help. Neal escaped out the driver's side. Farley died a few hours later of a gunshot wound to the stomach. Neal was caught and charged with first degree murder. Tulley was later caught in Nevada and provided state's evidence against Neal.

Neal was known by several aliases and had spent only eighteen years and seven months of his life outside of institutions. He had served time in Folsom and San Quentin. Married twice, both times to women who lived in Salt Lake City, he had come to Utah to see his son: "You may ask—why did I come here? I came here to see my son—whom I've never seen—even to date—and who knows nothing of me or that I am his father—which is as it should and will always be!"[13]

Neal maintained his innocence throughout his trial. While confined on death row, he wrote to the warden: "I

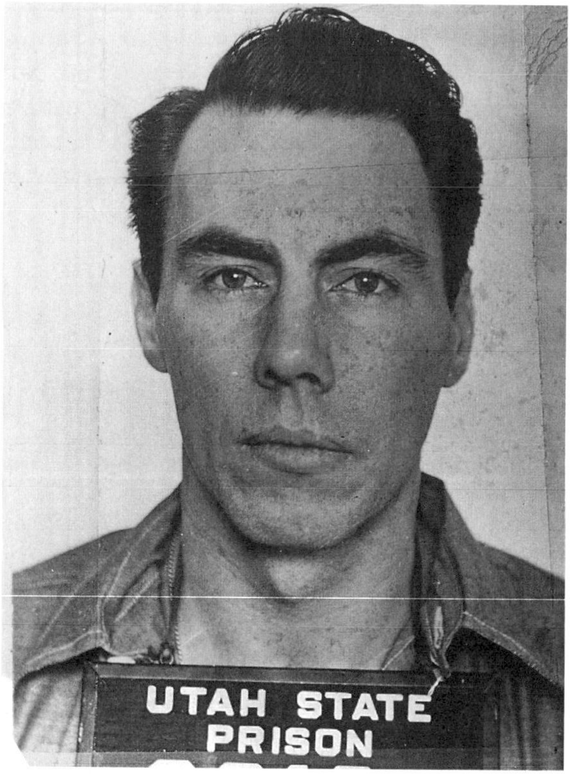

"Wilma, confess your crime or I will die." Don Jesse Neal executed on 1 July 1955.

didn't do it Warden—honest to God I didn't! I don't know what to say or what to look forward to and how to appeal for help—but please Warden believe me."[14] There were many who believed him. Shortly before his execution, an article in *Argosy* magazine opined: "Don Neal is partially the product of a system of penology founded on an erroneous fallacy. He is partially the product of his own environment, of his own thinking, and he may well have been a victim of one of the greatest injustices ever perpetrated by law."[15]

Neal's case dragged out in the courts. Stays were issued, new evidence and witnesses found, and appeals mounted from concerned citizens. In the meantime, Neal was signing contracts for a movie to be made of his life. He was a prolific correspondent. One woman even gave up her job in California and came to Utah to meet Neal and get him freed.

Neal contended that Tulley had killed the officer. Neal's hands were cuffed behind his back and he was sitting next to the policeman. The autopsy showed Farley had been shot in the stomach, the bullet entering just above the navel, traveling in a straight line, just grazing his backbone. Neal was searched before entering the car, and two officers searched the car prior to Neal and Tulley's return. According to Neal, the only person with access to a gun was Tulley, whose purse had not been searched. He claimed Tulley took the gun out of her purse and was seen by the officer, who lunged to grab the weapon. It went off into his abdomen.

Four weeks before his scheduled execution, Neal asked his aunt to put the following ad in the newspapers: "Wilma Tulley, for God's Sake write Governor, confess your crime or I will die July 1. Hurry don't let me die."[16] Whatever the truth, Neal was executed at the Utah State Prison on 1 July 1955.

* * *

On 22 October 1949 during an early morning robbery of a Standard service station in Beaver, Utah, Verne Alfred Braasch and Melvin Leroy Sullivan shot and killed the attendant, Howard W. (Duke) Manzione, one hour before the end of his shift. He was shot four times and died after being transported to the Cedar City Hospital.[17] Braasch and Sullivan were captured the next day in Las Vegas.

Tried and sentenced four times to die, they survived each execution date until 1956. They held the record at the time for being the longest on Utah's death row—six years. The process and the expense became so frustrating to Governor J. Bracken Lee that he submitted a bill to the U.S. Department of Justice for $19,685.12—$615.06 per month.

With all appeals exhausted, Braasch and Sullivan released a statement to the press shortly before their execution:

> In as much as we have only a few hours more to live . . . we wish to make a public statement. First, we do not protest against being punished. We are found guilty of a serious crime. In the second place, we wish to say, in partial excuse for ourselves, that we did not have a fair chance in life. Coming from broken homes, we grew up in neglect. In youth we were denied parental care, affection and guidance. Religious training would have pointed us in the right direction, but we were not taken to Sunday School or to church services. While in prison during the long years of waiting we have tried to build up in our souls what was lacking. We now try to accept our severe punishment with true religious resignation (*Deseret News and Telegram,* 11 May 1956).

Braasch and Sullivan ate their last meal of roast pheasant, green salad, and strawberries and cream. The warden in his memo authorizing the last meal also ordered "one pint each of dry wine and sweet wine to be shared between the inmates."[18]

Theirs was a double execution, the second in Utah's history; the first was that of Antelope and Longhair in 1854.

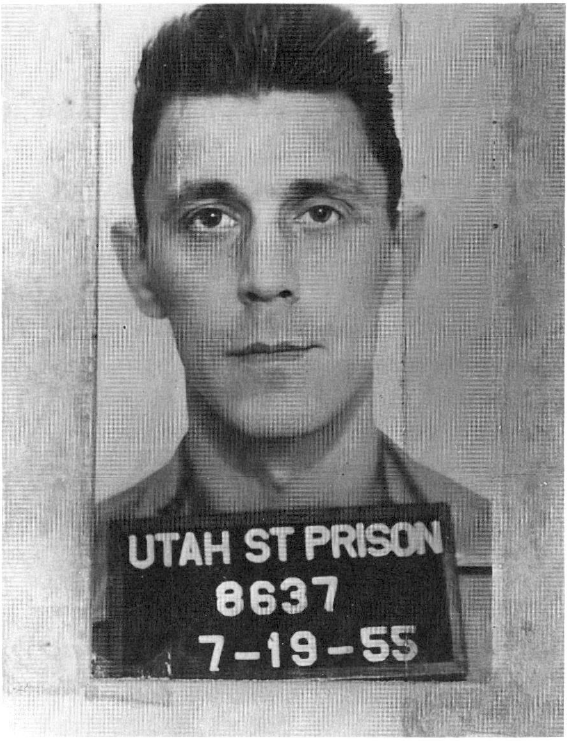

"Coming from broken homes, we grew up in neglect."
Verne Alfred Braasch executed with Melvin Sullivan
on 11 May 1956.

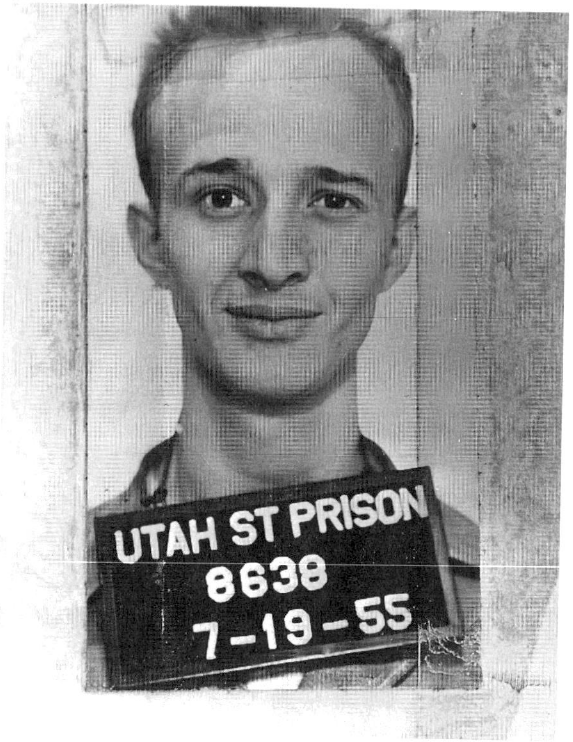

Melvin LeRoy Sullivan executed with Verne Braasch on 11 May 1956.

Scene of the Braasch and Sullivan double-execution by firing squad. Note one black chair and one white chair. Courtesy Utah State Historical Society.

Two hearses leaving the prison after the Braasch and Sullivan execution. Courtesy Utah State Historical Society.

The two chairs were placed on a sled-type apparatus. Sandbags were placed behind the chairs and wood shavings covered the floor. Two chairs were used—one black, which had been used for other executions, and one white, newly painted. Sullivan sat in the black one; Braasch in the white. The execution was conducted by the sheriff of Iron County, where the trial had been held. (The trial had been changed from Beaver County, because it was feared an impartial trial could not be conducted in the county where the crime occurred.) The sheriff placed his hat over his heart thus signalling the two separate firing squads to do their work. Both men were pronounced dead within one minute of the shots.

Manzione's father, along with "several hundred" other witnesses, was present at the execution. Afterwards he said: "Now perhaps we can have peace. We want everyone to know that we have never had any thought of revenge or malice toward anyone. We're just glad that at last it's over" (*Deseret News and Telegram,* 11 May 1956). The Catholic chaplain wrote to Braasch's mother, "Verne helped stabilize Melvin at the time of the execution." She wrote back requesting his help in finding a marker for her son's grave.

* * *

On 12 August 1956 Barton Kay Kirkham entered the Nibley Park Grocery Store, 501 East 2700 South in Salt Lake City, to buy a pack of cigarettes: "I entered the store only with the intention of holding up the storekeeper, but I knew he had more money than he had given me and I was mad because he had lied" (*Deseret News and Telegram,* 13 Aug. 1956). He forced the storekeeper, David Avon Frame, into the back apartment of the store, where Mrs. Ruth Webster was polishing a pair of shoes for her daughter: "I forced them into the bathroom, laid them down on the floor and . . . when they moved on the floor, I shot them" (ibid.). Frame and Webster were tending the store for the owners, Ervin Holmes and his wife, who were vacationing in Boise, Idaho.

Later, at about midnight, Kirkham forced a car with

three teenage boys in it to the side of the road. He asked them why they were following him. When they denied they were, he told them to get out but allowed them to drive on when another car approached. The boys left and reported the incident to a policeman.

A half an hour later Kirkham kidnapped a sister and brother, seventeen-year-old Shawna Lou Christean and twenty-one-year old Arthur Christean, and forced them to drive him up Provo Canyon. The brother was released from the car, and Kirkham and the girl continued to drive until 4:30 a.m. when the Utah Highway Patrol received a call from Kirkham at a pay phone: "I'm up Provo Canyon and I have a girl in the car and I want you to pick me up before I cause more trouble. Turn your red lights on for identification. I won't cause you any trouble when you come" (*Deseret News and Telegram,* 13 Aug. 1956).

Kirkham had joined the Air Force as a jet mechanic at the age of seventeen. In England he was disciplined for "shacking up" and returned to Mountain Home Air Force Base in Idaho. While AWOL from there, he committed armed robbery and was sentenced to the Colorado Reformatory at Buena Vista for nine months. He was released to his parents' custody on 31 May 1956—two and a half months before the Nibley Market murders.

Kirkham was tried, found guilty, and sentenced to die. "I chose hanging," he later maintained, "instead of the firing squad because of the publicity . . . the novelty . . . to put the state to more inconvenience." He was the sixth and last person hanged in Utah.

Before his death Kirkham wrote:

> There was so much hate in me then and it keeps building up and there was no release for it, and I did not care what happened. The Doctors said I felt justified when I killed those people and they are right. I did. It was revenge I was after. The love that

"I did kill those people to hurt my parents." Barton Kay Kirkham executed on 7 July 1958.

> I was denied because my parents spent so much time doing church work and they still do, and forcing me to stay home and lead the life they wanted me to live. I got my revenge and I am not sorry now and never will be. . . . I've had enough of it, I want to die. I'm fed up with it all. I did kill those people to hurt my parents and their good standing in the church. Who failed me it was not only my parents but myself and a lot of others. My life is a real mess now, and I will be glad when it is all over with.[19]

* * *

On 19 June 1957 while working at the Rattlesnake uranium mine near La Sal, Utah, James W. Rodgers shot and killed Charles Merrifield, a fellow employee. There had been an on-going dispute between the two, and Rodgers claimed he had been threatened on several occasions. On this particular day Rodgers had been told Merrifield was going to "beat him up." After further agitation, Rodgers "challenged Merrifield with a gun." When Merrifield came after him with a large wrench, Rodgers shot him.

Rodgers was the oldest of eleven children. He left home at the age of twelve. His father only knew hard work and did not allow his children time for play. Rodgers had been in several prisons and had spent a total of twenty-three years behind bars prior to his final conviction. Both legs were scarred from machine gun bullets dating back to his "work" with bootleggers in Missouri at the age of sixteen.

To this murder in Utah, he pleaded "guilty by reason of insanity," claiming he had syphilis. After receiving the death penalty, he stated he was not concerned about his execution because he believed he would die of syphilis before he could be executed. Prison tests and tests by other experts did not confirm that he had syphilis.

While on death row he was a model inmate. Prior to his execution he wrote to prison officials, "Friends of the Institution": "I will try to convey to you, One and All, Both Inmates

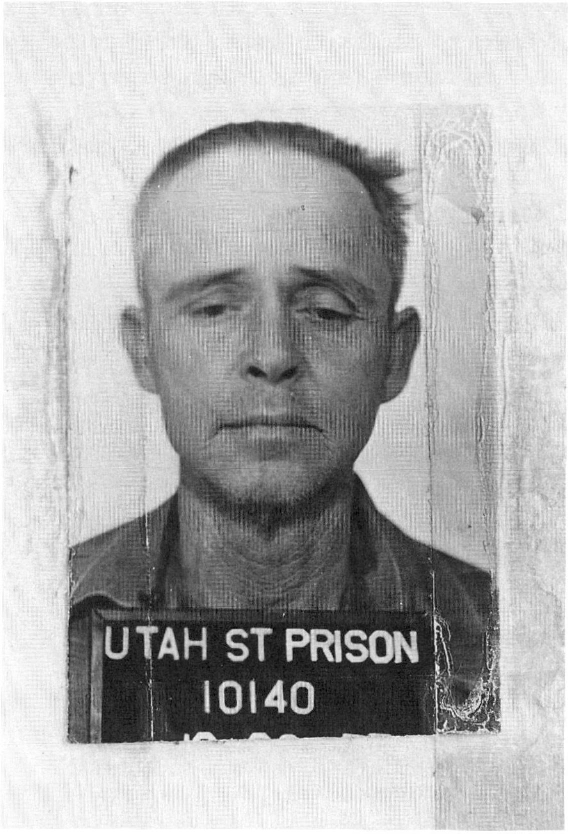

"Guilty by reason of syphilis." James W. Rodgers executed on 30 March 1960.

and personal [sic], my deepest gratitude for the many favors and the kindness which you extended to me, in the last 2 years. I also wish you one and all the very best of everything."[20] Rodgers was executed 30 March 1960.

After his execution his mother wrote to the chaplain:

> I gave him a nice burial even tho I am a widow with $90.00 per month to pay for it. I could not see him buried in Potter's field. . . . I know his soul is in heaven with God and I will meet him someday and hope to meet all of you up there.
>
> will say so long to all
> I am one more mother
> who has had her son
> executed there.
> God Bless All.[21]

NOTES

1. Original letter in Utah State Prison files (hereafter USPF).
2. Original letter in USPF.
3. Original letter to the Board of Pardons, 11 Oct. 1938, in USPF.
4. Quoted in *Life Magazine,* 14 Oct. 1938, 20.
5. Copy of affidavit in USPF.
6. Letter to Governor Maw and the Board of Pardons, 12 June 1942, in USPF.
7. An interesting footnote is that the sentencing judge was Lewis V. Trueman, one of the victims of the next man to be executed in Utah—Austin Cox also from Weber County.
8. Transcript of evidence hearing, 1-3 Sept. 1943, #4191, Second Judicial District.
9. Original letter to the Board of Pardons, 14 June 1945, in USPF.
10. Mares's handwritten statement, in USPF.
11. Lee Green, "Women Seem to Trust Me," 73

12. Original letter in USPF.

13. Neal, "I Am Innocent," 1 June 1955, in USPF.

14. Note to Warden Marcell Graham, 28 March 1953, in USPF.

15. Erle Stanley Gardner, "The Strange Case of Don Jesse Neal," *Argosy*, Aug. 1955

16. Ad submitted by Neal's "Aunt Grace" at his request, *Oregonian*, June 1955.

17. Howard (Duke) Manzione was buried in Mountain View Cemetery in Beaver. He had been married two months at the time of his death. The summer after his death, his bride gave birth to a baby boy. She later remarried. The service station in which Manzione died has been demolished and a new Board of Education building occupies the corner. Manzione's son is now a merchant in southern Utah.

18. Warden's memo, in USPF.

19. Letter to a woman in Idaho, copy in my possession, courtesy of George S. Tanner.

20. Original letter, 19 March 1960, in USPF.

21. Original letter, in USPF.

6.

MODERN EXECUTIONS

On 2 June 1967 Luis Monge was executed by hanging at the Colorado state prison for killing his wife. Monge's would be the last execution in the United States until ten years later when the state of Utah executed Gary Gilmore. An unofficial nationwide moratorium on executions was observed beginning in 1967, and all executions ceased. Five years later, on 29 June 1972, in its 5-4 Furman v. Georgia decision, the U.S. Supreme Court struck down the capital punishment laws of thirty-five states, sparing the lives of over six hundred men and two women awaiting execution on death rows across the country.

At the time of this decision five men were awaiting execution in Utah:

Darrell Devere Poulsen, age thirty-one, had been sentenced to die for raping and killing eleven-year-old Karen Ann Mechling of American Fork on 17 September 1961. Her father found her body under a tree in a vacant lot near the apartment building where she had been babysitting. Poulsen was arrested, tried, convicted, and sentenced to death.

He entered the Utah state prison on 26 December 1961.

Myron Daryl Lance, age twenty-five, and Walter Bernard Kelbach, age twenty-eight, had both been sentenced to die for a killing spree during the week before Christmas in December 1966. Five people were killed in five days before the arrest of Lance and Kelbach in Parley's Canyon. The victims included two male service station attendants, a cab driver, and two patrons of Lally's Tavern in Salt Lake City. Both Lance and Kelbach had been released on parole from the Utah state prison just a few months before the killings.

Bennett Merle Belwood, supposedly accompanied by Ruth Ruby Bruce, killed Ronald Paul Smith at Big Hollow Canyon near Dugway by shooting him twice from behind. Belwood confessed to the killing, claiming he and his partner were like Bonnie and Clyde, and referred to the crime as a "Glory Sweep." He pleaded innocent by reason of insanity but was found guilty of first degree murder. The jury did not recommend leniency, and he was sentenced to die by hanging. His original conviction was overturned, he was retried after the moratorium, and was found guilty again but this time was sentenced to life in prison.

Clark James Redford was serving time for forgery in the Utah state prison when he was arrested and returned to Eureka, Utah, for trial in the murder of Ann Levanger. Her body was found in the central Utah desert, where she had been raped and strangled. Redford had picked her up along the freeway after her car stalled. He was sentenced to death by firing squad on 10 September 1970 and given an execution date of 23 October 1970.

Of these five only Lance and Kelbach remain today in prison. They were resentenced in 1967 to two consecutive life sentences. Poulsen, Belwood, and Redford have all since been released. One of them has a new name; the others have families, sometimes jobs, and go about their daily activities for the most part unnoticed.

Not until 27 November 1974 were there any new residents of Utah's death row. On that date Dale Pierre (who later changed his name to Pierre Dale) Selby and William Andrews entered the prison. They were to be followed by Gary Gilmore.

* * *

While on parole from the federal prison in Marion, Illinois, Gary Mark Gilmore entered a Sinclair station in Provo, robbed the attendant, Max David Jensen, then forced him into the bathroom and killed him with two shots to the head. The next night he robbed and killed Bennie Bushnell at the City Motel. While trying to dispose of the gun in some bushes, it went off, injuring his hand. He was later spotted by a service station attendant and was captured that same night.

Gilmore's execution was the first in the United States following the Furman decision. During the years after 1972, the U.S. Supreme Court in a series of cases had reaffirmed the constitutionality of the death penalty and set forth specific guidelines for its application. Had Gilmore chosen to fight execution, he could have drawn the process out for several years. Instead, he preferred death to the type of life he had already experienced in prisons, reform schools, and institutions in Idaho, Oregon, California, Texas, Washington, and Illinois. He first entered the justice system at the age of twelve when he was described as "spoiled, headstrong and hostile toward authority figures."[1]

Gilmore was the second of four children. His father had been married previously, his mother had not. One psychiatrist noted, "He was overindulged by his mother, his father was gone most of the time and the family moved a lot."[2]

Gilmore was disruptive in prison, and he received numerous write-ups for abusive language, spitting, throwing food, and so on. Following a failed suicide attempt, he bit and spit in the face of one of the nurses. At one point he

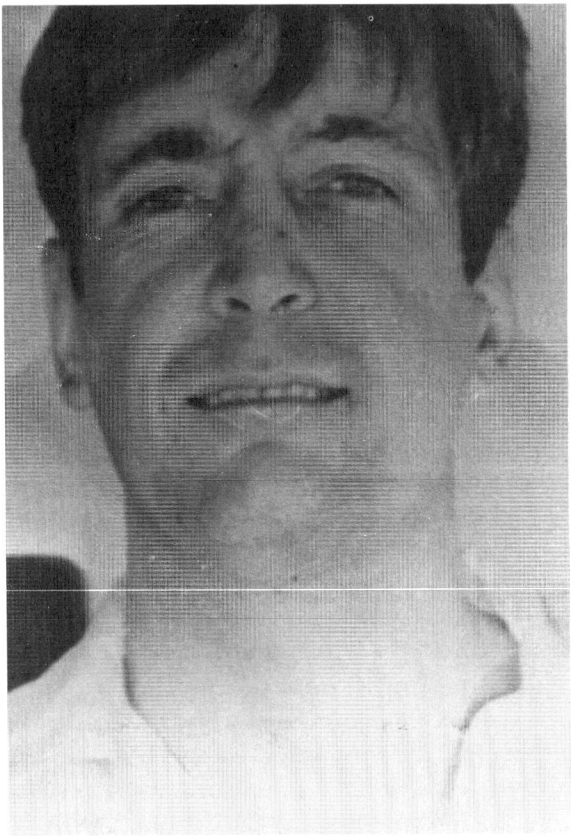

"Your shots didn't kill Gary . . . his life did." Gary Mark Gilmore executed on 17 January 1977.

stated to those attending him: "If the state of Utah did not have the 'guts' to shoot him he would continue to try to take his own life." He bragged that he would be successful even if it meant biting off his tongue and bleeding to death.[3]

Prior to his execution he ordered no special meal, only "regular prison fare." His last request—"I would like to drink a few tall Coors, maybe a six-pack, if possible"[4]—was not granted. Early in the morning of 17 January 1977, Gilmore was strapped into an old office chair, a small black target with a white circle placed over his heart, and a black hood placed over his head. At 8:07 a.m. he was pronounced dead, the first indoor execution in Utah since 1951 and the first execution in the U.S. since 1967.

After Gilmore's execution, his uncle, aunt, and two cousins wrote the following note to prison officials: "I would like to express my feelings, also my families', to you. I don't know how you feel or what might be going on inside you. But I would like you to know, speaking for all of us, we hold no hard feelings in any way, concerning Gary Gilmore. It is something that had to be. It was also what Gary wanted. Your shots didn't kill Gary Gilmore, his LIFE did. I hope you take this as a feeling from our hearts."[5]

Gilmore's life was recounted in a book by Norman Mailer and in a Hollywoood television movie *Executioner's Song,* and in his brother Mikel's book, *Shot in the Heart.* Utah's first execution after 1967 was followed by executions in Nevada of Jesse Bishop in 1978 and in Florida of John Spinkelink in 1979.

* * *

Prior to closing time on 22 April 1974, Dale Pierre, William Andrews, and Keith Roberts drove past the Ogden Hi-Fi Shop at 2323 Washington Boulevard. Pierre and Andrews got out of the car a block down the street; Roberts remained in the vehicle and drove to the back door of the Hi-Fi Shop.

Pierre and Andrews entered the shop and began looking around, preparing to rob the store. Before the night was over, three people would be killed—Carol Naisbitt, 52; Michelle Ansley, 19; and Stanley Walker, 20. All were forced to drink a caustic drain cleanser and then shot; Ansley had been raped. Two others—Orren Walker, 43, and Cortney Naisbitt, 16—survived. Walker also had a ball point pen kicked into his ear. Three days later, Pierre, Andrews, and Roberts, all in the Air Force, were arrested and charged with murder.

At the trial, Pierre and Andrews were tried together. Roberts was given a separate trial, found guilty of two counts of aggravated robbery, and sentenced to prison. Pierre and Andrews were found guilty of first degree murder and sentenced to death by firing squad.

Roberts served thirteen years and was paroled in May 1987 while preparations were being made for the execution of Pierre. Some believed it was actually Roberts who planned the Hi-Fi robbery, but that was never established.

While in prison, Dale Pierre changed his name to Pierre Dale Selby to avoid further embarrassment for his family. Selby and Andrews spent thirteen years on death row together. It was expected they would die together in Utah's first double execution since Braasch and Sullivan in 1956. However, their appeals became separated in 1987, when the U.S. Supreme Court turned down Selby's appeal and the tenth circuit court became reinvolved in Andrews's appeal.

Selby appeared before Judge Wahlquist for resentencing on 7 July. He refused to choose between firing squad and lethal injection and was sentenced to die 28 August by lethal injection. Hanging had been outlawed in 1980. On 13 August Selby appeared before the board of pardons in an attempt to have his sentence commuted. During two days of testimony, the board considered Selby's plea:

> I have often thought that if my death would restore the victims to life, then let's carry out the sentence, but it doesn't work that way. . . . also if it

> would stop the hurt, but it just doesn't work like that. My death would be just another death. . . . Anyway I would like to try to convince this Board my life is worth being spared, that there is something there worth saving. All I can offer is my sincere apologies the crime ever happened.[6]

The board also received a letter written by the mother of Michelle Ansley: "I once had a very loving, caring, beautiful daughter—my only daughter. . . . It is very difficult writing this letter because of the ache in my heart and the tears in my eyes get in the way. How much longer must I relive my daughter's death?"[7]

The Board of Pardons refused to commute Selby's sentence, issuing its ruling on 21 August at 11:30 a.m.: "Without assigning specific weight to each of the three areas of inquiry [circumstances of the crime; history of the offender and efforts at rehabilitation; the circumstances surrounding the penalty], the Board finds on balance that the petitioner has not met the burden required of him. Petitioner's request for commutation is denied."[8]

Shortly before his death Selby talked about the killings:

> The crime took a course of its own. It wasn't planned that way. People kept coming in and I just panicked. The only way to prevent what happened was to have been moved away from the Air Force entirely . . . Of course the alcohol and the pills I was consuming didn't help—valiums, reds, black beauties and yellow jackets. Everyone has a limit beyond which they won't go—drugs, etc., can alter that limit. I tell myself, "You have to accept responsibility for it—you did it, you were there. You can't rationalize it" (interview).

Selby was executed on 28 August 1987, the first in Utah

by lethal injection. He spent his last twenty-four hours fasting, reading the Bible, and completing Seventh-day Adventist reading assignments and lessons. He was calm, conversed with his minister and attorneys prior to execution, and then lay down on the gurney in the execution chamber. He was pronounced dead at 1:13 a.m. He was secretly buried in Salt Lake City.

His death was described by the *Salt Lake Tribune* on 29 August 1987:

> Lying face up, clad in a white jump suit and bound to a gurney with heavy leather straps, Selby lay motionless in the brightly lit white room. . . .
>
> The tan-colored gurney was mounted on a steel pedestal bolted to the floor near a pane of one-way glass. From a small square hole beneath the window ran two plastic tubes that disappeared into white towels wrapped around each of Selby's outstretched arms. . . .
>
> The warden broke the spell by stepping to Selby's side, leaning over and speaking to him. The sound of his voice did not penetrate to the witness room, but we knew the warden was asking Selby if he had any last words.
>
> Selby moved his head slightly to the left and mouthed something. The warden spoke again; Selby replied. The exchange took 30 seconds or so, during which Selby flexed the index fingers on both hands slowly and stretched his feet forward and back slightly.
>
> The warden stepped away, stopped about 15 feet from Selby and gave a nod toward the executioner's room. . . .
>
> And we knew that unseen, behind the one-way mirror, two executioners were pushing the plungers on the first of three syringes. One executioner was

Pierre Dale Selby as he appeared before the board of pardons prior to his execution. L. Kay Gillespie is in the background between Selby and his attorney, Gil Athay. Courtesy *Deseret News*.

now injecting sodium pentothal, a powerful anesthetic, into the tube that would carry it to Selby's bloodstream. The other executioner's syringe was filled with a harmless saline solution.

Two more chemicals would be injected into Selby, one at a time, over the next few minutes. Next would be Pavulon, a muscle relaxant that would stop his lungs from working. The last, potassium chloride, would stop his heart.

As the chemicals began to flow, Selby lay very still beneath a harsh fluorescent lamp hanging directly above his head. He licked his lips twice and his eyelids fluttered briefly. Thirty seconds later, Selby appeared to have fallen asleep. . . .

Now the only sign of life in Selby's body was a heartbeat evidenced by a quick pulsing movement beneath the jump suit near the area of his upper stomach. About three minutes later, his heart also stopped.

* * *

Over a five-year period beginning in 1979, five young boys from the Salt Lake County area mysteriously disappeared. The first was a four-year-old, the last a thirteen-year-old. Three of the victims were found buried in Cedar Valley, the other two were located in a log jam in Big Cottonwood Canyon. Arthur Gary Bishop confessed to all five killings while being questioned about the disappearance of the last boy. He had sexually molested all five, then killed them to keep them from telling. He was tried, found guilty, and on 23 March 1984 was sentenced to die by lethal injection.

Bishop had been a high school honor student, an Eagle Scout, and a Mormon missionary. At the time of his confession, he stated: "I've done a wrong to society here; I've killed their children that I've loved sometimes and . . . there's no way that I can bring them back, there's no way that I can really comfort their parents. . . . I wake up nights with nightmares sometimes. I was afraid they'd be waiting any time in the dark for me" (*Salt Lake Tribune,* 10 June 1988, and my interviews).

Bishop, like Gary Gilmore, wanted to die. The guilt he lived with was intolerable. In response to a question from a group of teenagers, Bishop responded: "I feel that I . . . will serve my time in hell for what I have done. I feel strongly that there are mitigating circumstances which will affect my salvation. Honestly, I don't totally understand why I did what I did. No man on this earth can give me a fair judgement. . . . The knowledge of my crimes often drags my soul through torment; to some extent I have already begun my time in hell."[10] Bishop dismissed his attorneys in order to expedite his execution. In a May 1988 interview with him he said, "I have messed up this life; I am anxious to get on with what needs to be done in the next one."

On 8 June 1988 at 7:42 p.m. the process of execution began. Bishop was taken from his maximum security cell, strip searched, cuffed, and dressed in orange coveralls. He stood quietly with his head down—speaking only to offer assistance to those dressing him in the coveralls. At 7:58 p.m. Bishop arrived at the death watch cell, where he would be under constant visual supervision awaiting his 10 June execution. By 8:00 he was going through the housekeeping ritual that seems to preoccupy all inmates as they change cells—making the bed, washing the sink, arranging items in the cell—putting their personal mark on their territory.

While under death watch supervision, the condemned inmate is observed constantly, awake or sleeping. A continuous log is kept by each officer. The death watch log for Bishop documents his last hours of life:

JUNE 8, 1988

7:57 p.m. Bishop escorted to the Execution Building. Bishop cooperative during this operation. Placed into Death Watch Cell at 8:07p.m.

9:12 p.m.	Inmate Bishop reading the Book of Mormon. Continued reading until 11:20 p.m.
11:20 p.m.	Inmate Bishop made bed. Went to sleep at midnight.

JUNE 9, 1988

12:01 a.m.	Inmate Bishop sleeping with towel over his eyes to shade the lights. Continues to sleep until 5:30 a.m. . . .
7:20 a.m.	Inmate Bishop reading Book of Mormon and praying. Very quiet.
7:30 a.m.	Inmate Bishop refused breakfast. Stated he was fasting. Continued reading until 8:45 a.m. . . .
10:08 a.m.	Inmate Bishop still talking to [visitor] about the Book or Mormon and life after death.
12:28 p.m.	Inmate Bishop was asked if he would like lunch. Bishop said "no." . . .
1:49 p.m.	Jay Lowe, LDS bishop, visits with Bishop. Bishop talks about feeling at peace; says he is not afraid to die; he also talks to Mr. Lowe about funeral services. . . .
3:30 p.m.	Bishop is lying on his bunk and reading the Book of Mormon.
4:00 p.m.	Bishop continues to read the Book of Mormon. . . .
6:20 p.m.	Inmate Bishop talkative. Appears to be in a good mood.
6:25 p.m.	Inmate Bishop requested and received [Book of Mormon, Doctrine and Covenants, and Pearl of Great Price]. Inmate Bishop lying on bunk reading. . . .
11:02 p.m.	Bishop asked Heber Geurts to give him some time alone to pray. Mr. Geurts leaves the Death Watch area.
11:04 p.m.	Bishop lays down on his bed.

11:18 p.m. Warden Cook goes in to speak with Bishop. Bishop was praying and did not talk with the Warden nor was Bishop interrupted from his prayer. . . .

11:42 p.m. Bishop was escorted to the Execution Chamber.

At 11:50 p.m. Bishop was strapped to the gurney, his legs and thighs quivering. He licked his dry lips. Just after leaving the death watch cell he told me, "I did pretty good until about five minutes ago. Now my nerves are gone." At 12:08 a.m. the lethal doses began. I watched his chest slowly rise and fall. Then there was nothing. He was pronounced dead at 12:15 a.m. In his last visit with his parents he told them, "In the quiet moments, be still and if I can I'll come to you and let you know I am all right."

The mother of his last victim said: "My anger has had an avenue, I could see the system, make it work, will it to work. But what do you do with all that without any excuse? Tell me . . . I don't know how to let go with any of it. After he's [Bishop] gone, it's all up to me. It's a hell of a lot to face. I'm afraid" (*Salt Lake Tribune,* 10 June 1988). The father of another of his victims said: "It is one thing to lose a child in an accident. But to have one disappear is more torment than a person can endure. . . . All I can do is try to cope. . . . Try to get through every day. . . . It is never gone" (ibid.).

One of Bishop's last acts was to give me a letter he had written to a young man who had been sexually molesting children:

> With all my heart I urge you to continue faithfully in repenting. Stop and think about the spiritual damage you've already inflicted upon some very choice souls. How do you think they feel about what you've done? It's good that you've stopped molesting children, but what would happen if you lost self-con-

> trol and started again? Eventually you would be caught. You would go to court and probably to prison. You would have disgraced yourself and your family. In prison you would be considered one of the least desirable of criminals and catcalls of "rapo," "low-life," "baby raper," "sicko," and "pervert," would follow you. Your past is thrown unmercifully into your face, and you are never allowed to forget what you've done. Inmates can be cruel, and they are very slow to acknowledge any repentance efforts or change on your part. Is this the kind of life you want for yourself? I of all people have the least right to lecture you, and I sadly realize that the best advice I can give you is *not* to follow my bad example. Learn from my mistakes.[12]

At the time of Bishop's execution eight men remained on Utah's death row: William Andrews, Elroy Tilman, Ronnie Lee Gardner, Douglas S. Carter, Ralph Menzies, James Lewis Holland, Joseph Mitchell Parsons, and Ron Lafferty. In response to a question from my students at Weber State College after the Selby and Bishop executions, William Andrews wrote:

> When Selby was executed I did not hear about it until the next morning over the radio. I guess my first reaction was an emotional disbelief with an intellectual acceptance of the fact. . . . I think it was maybe an hour or so later that my emotional self beg[a]n to accept the fact that Selby was dead. At this point I became very sad. . . . I had come to know Selby as a kind and giveing [sic] person to me and anyone else that would give him the opportunity to be h[i]mself. . . . Over the years we had come to be like brothers and now he was dead. I couldn't help thinking of the people that died at the Hi Fi Shop and how

"I have messed up this life . . . I am anxious to get on with the next." Arthur Gary Bishop executed on 10 June 1988.

> stupid and senseless their deaths were also and the sorrow their loved ones must of went throu[gh] also. And I knew that with Selby's death the killing would not stop.[13]

Andrews was given an execution date of 22 August 1989. On 10 August he was granted a commutation hearing before the board of pardons. He pointed out that he was not convicted of killing anyone and should not be executed. The board refused Andrews's appeal, but on 20 August, only two days before the execution, a federal circuit court of appeals issued a 160-day stay of execution. On 30 July 1992, Andrews became the second man executed in Utah who did not actually kill someone.

* * *

I walked with William Andrews as he was led into the execution chamber. He was helped onto the gurney, and the tie-down team began strapping him down. With his last free arm he took off his glasses and, handing them to one of the men, remarked, "I guess I won't need these anymore." At that moment I could hear the telephone ringing in the area where the executioners were stationed. Lane McCotter, Executive Director of the Department of Corrections, stepped through the door and informed Andrews that the U.S. Supreme Court had requested a temporary delay while they considered several questions. He told Andrews that he would be returned to the death watch cell until further word was received.

I cannot imagine what must go through a person's mind who, having reconciled himself to his fate and being only minutes from death, is then unstrapped and returned to await the whole process again.

I followed Andrews back to his cell and thought he might want to talk. He sat on his bed, his blanket wrapped around his shoulders, staring at the opposite wall. He didn't want to talk to anyone.

I had known Andrews for more than eight years. We met when I began my interviews on death row. He was the most willing to talk. We spent many hours together talking about everything from his life to his death—but very seldom about his crime. We corresponded regularly and, on a couple occasions, he answered written questions from my students at Weber State University. To one asking if he had found any purpose or hope during his years on death row, he responded: "Yes. . . . It may not be much but it helps me to feel good about myself and it helps also. What I do is, in my interpersonal relationships, here with the other inmates I try to encourage them to learn self control, have more self respect, and to have a more positive attitude about themselves, other people and life in general."

He did, as a matter of fact, have the most positive attitude of all the men I visited on death row. He continually reminded me of his philosophy: "Where there's life, there's hope." He was disappointed when Art Bishop withdrew his appeals and prepared to die, believing that he should have kept trying to save his life.

During the last few weeks prior to his execution, Andrews became despondent. In his last letter to me, dated 5 March 1992, he wrote: "I haven't been in the mood to do a lot of reading lately. My concentration hasn't been good enough to do any serious reading. Its hard to keep ones interest in things related to the living when you are stareing death in the face. Almost everything seems irrelevant. Seems like I am just passing time until that fateful day. I haven't given up, just put everything on hold until I know for sure if I will live or die."

That "fateful day" arrived in late July. Andrews was transferred from maximum security to the death watch on 28 July 1992 at 2304 hours. During the next twenty-four hours the clock would wind down on a predetermined schedule. Andrews would be under constant surveillance and, outside the institution, the components necessary to conduct an execution would begin to move into place:

1600	Security sweeps begin at the execution chamber and move outward.
1700	A general briefing takes place at the Training Center, where the news media begins to set up.
1800	Command Post operational sets up, including roadblocks, crowd control, and security.
2000	All posts begin hourly radio check-ins.

While the department's official machinery was being coordinated, Andrews began his last meal—a huge banana split, which he had requested. When it arrived, it was so large he was allowed to have his sister and niece, who were visiting, join him in his cell and share it. They ate and talked, even laughing at times as they remembered former friends, school experiences, and family memories. Both his sister and niece were present as invited witnesses at the execution.

The Supreme Court delay lasted about an hour. When advised that the state could proceed, a new time was set for 0135. At 0116 Andrews was returned to the execution chamber where he was strapped down and then waited for various witnesses—his invited witnesses, media representatives, and government witnesses. As I stood with the government witnesses, I could hear Andrews talking with warden Scott Carver. I later learned that he was recommending they pipe in music and commission a painting for the ceiling so that the condemned would have something to listen to and look at. He suggested one of the scenes they showed in the movie *Soylent Green*, a film that depicted the voluntary euthanizing of the elderly.

William Andrews "Hi-Fi Killer" executed 30 July 1992.

When the curtains were drawn back for the witnesses, Andrews raised his head and mouthed, "I love you," to his sister and niece. At 01:34 he was asked if he had any last words, these were given and, one minute later, the warden unbuttoned his jacket as a signal to begin. Andrews took several deep breaths, his head moved back and forth two or three times and I could see bubbles moving through the tubes attached to the needles in his wrists. He was pronounced dead at 01:46.

His last words were: "Thank those who tried so hard to keep me alive. Tell them to keep fighting for equal justice and tell my family that I love them." Thus ended an eighteen-year nightmare that began on 22 April 1974 with the botched robbery of the Ogden Hi-Fi Shop at 2323 Washington Boulevard and ended with the execution of William Andrews.

The Hi-Fi Shop has been replaced with a modern shopping mall, and most of the young people growing up today in Ogden and the surrounding area have little sense of the anger, frustration, and evil that surrounded this crime and the community hatred that continued to fester as long as the "Hi-Fi killers" were alive. Every new appeal, date of execution, and hearing revived smoldering resentment. One anonymous letter Andrews received shortly before his execution symbolizes that resentment:

> Your death will rid society of the threat you mad dogs pose to society. . . . And the law and the people have condemned you to death—proved you guilty beyond all doubt.
>
> Trying to oily mouth your way out of your guilt makes you not only a murdering, conscienceless monster, but a whining wimp who expects to do as he pleases without taking the consequences. You *will* be executed—too bad it can only be once.

The next execution also came from Weber County.

* * *

On the day John Albert Taylor was executed in Utah, Delaware had scheduled an execution by hanging and Illinois was preparing to kill a woman who would have become the first woman executed in the U.S. since North Carolina's Velma Barfield in 1984. In spite of these other newsworthy events, the focus of national and international attention was on Taylor, whose execution would be carried out by firing squad—the first since Gary Gilmore's execution in 1977.

Why this interest? Because of the firing squad. The "medicalization" of the death penalty through lethal injection became popular because it assuaged the conscience of a guilty nation. Also of interest was the Mormon concept of "blood atonement," which surfaces every time there is a Utah execution. The firing squad is the only method of execution used in the U.S. that actually involves a "bloody" death, and Utah is the only state that uses the firing squad.

On 23 June 1989 Charla King's mother discovered her daughter's naked body on the floor of their apartment in Washington Terrace, a neighboring community of Ogden City in Weber County. She had been raped and strangled with a telephone cord and her panties had been stuffed into her mouth. She was one day shy of her twelfth birthday. Five days later John Albert Taylor, a thirty-year-old Florida parolee, was arrested. He was living with his sister in a neighboring apartment, and it was her suspicions that first brought Taylor to the attention of the police. His fingerprints were found on the telephone from which the cord that strangled Charla had been cut. Taylor admitted he had been in the King apartment, but only to rob it. He claimed no knowledge of the killing.

Taylor's police record dated back to his adolescence. His sister, who turned him in, admitted to having been raped by him when she was a child. There were other instances of sexual misconduct as well. In addition, Taylor had been previously charged with robberies, assaults, carrying a concealed weapon, sexual assault and battery, armed burglary, and armed robbery. He was incarcerated in the Florida State Prison at Broward in 1982, and had only recently returned to Ogden. Speaking of his past, Taylor told the *Salt Lake Tribune* on 26 January 1996: "When I raped or molested, it was a way for me to get back at the female race . . . Sex was one way for me to release the feelings I was going through. But I didn't know how to express them so I would go out and do something deviant or I would use alcohol or drugs to get the same effect." He maintained his innocence to the end. Shortly before his execution, however, he told me, "Sometimes I'm sorry I didn't take the plea bargain I was offered."

Taylor seemed comfortable on death row. He did art work and meditation for mental escape and used his prison job to buy "luxuries." Because of the nature of his crime, he was not liked by other inmates. Utah keeps its condemned in the same unit as other maximum security inmates, not on a separate "death row." In his section, for example, Taylor was the only one serving a death sentence. He told me, "I feel like I am in a day care center." The other inmates kept their distance as word spread that "He has nothing to lose, you're a damn fool if you push him." On the other hand, Taylor felt pressure because of his "death row status"—"I can't afford to back down," he told me. At the time of my interview, he had been in prison five and a half years and his health had "constantly gone down hill." He was afraid of dying alone in his cell. "Some days I wonder why I keep going," he complained. A few months later he got tired of holding on and stopped his appeals. He told me he opted for the firing squad because "It is symbolic to me. I maintain my innocence. If they put a bullet in me they are murdering me. It is the most hassle and the most expensive." Taylor told others he did not want to just lie there and "flop around like a fish." This was a

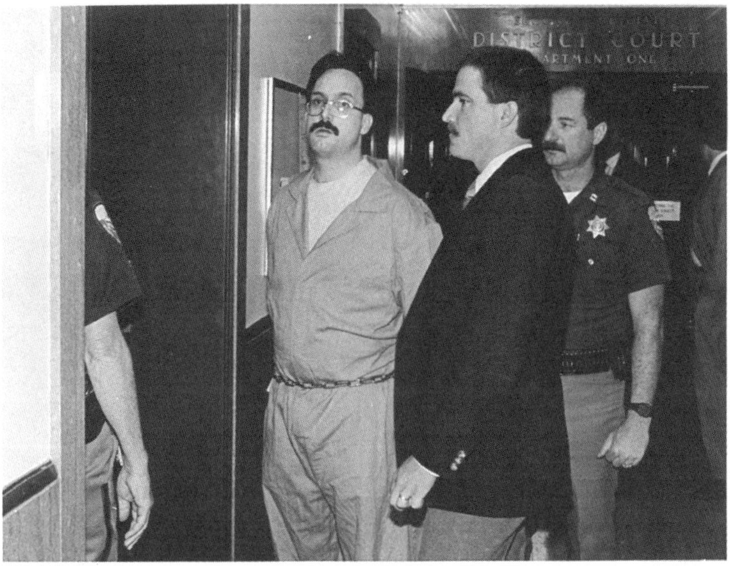

John Albert Taylor executed by firing squad 26 January 1996.

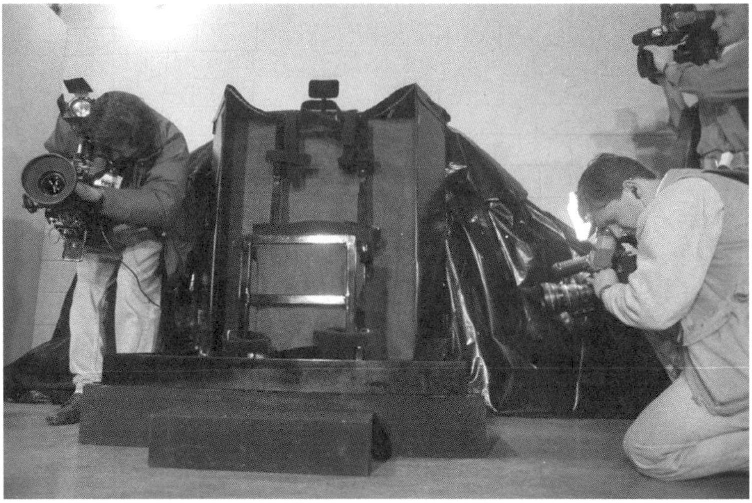

Reporters examining chair to be used in firing squad execution of John Albert Taylor.

consistent theme among the condemned men I have interviewed. For them it was important to "die game," not to show weakness or emotion. Many felt that lethal injection robbed them of their masculinity and "dignity" and that the firing squad, at least, allowed them to maintain both.

On 25 January 1996, his last full day, John Albert Taylor ate his last meal—a pizza with everything and a Coke. He also requested a last cigarette although the prison had a no smoking policy.

I was allowed to witness the execution as a government witness. We entered the execution area and positioned ourselves along the curtained windows. The time was 2400 (midnight). As the curtains opened, Taylor was already strapped to the chair and was looking directly at us. He continued to look at us as he was blindfolded. He sat motionless as he was asked if he had any final words. He expressed love to his family and friends and then stated, "I would just like to say to my family, my friends, as the poem was written, 'Remember me, but let me go.'" I next heard a voice say, "Ready—Aim—1-2-3," followed by one loud bang, four live rounds and one blank. The white target pinned to his dark blue jumpsuit flew off his chest. His body lurched, his hands clenched and unclenched twice, and he was still. I looked for blood but could see none. Others said they saw a dark discoloration on his jumpsuit where the bullets entered. From start to finish it had taken four minutes to execute John Albert Taylor. The curtains were released and we were escorted to the van and driven back to the training academy.

Because of the media attention, there had been an attempt in the Utah legislature, in session at the time of the execution, to eliminate the use of firing squad as an option. Once the execution was completed, however, and those involved with the execution saw how smoothly the process worked, the legislation was withdrawn.

My own observation is that the firing squad is a viable

option as a method of execution. I cannot say if it is more humane, although those who have been shot or wounded tell me there is an adrenaline surge or something that numbs the pain. From my experience, it takes less time and provides an appropriate setting for a process intended to mete out a sanction imposed by the justice system. Unlike lethal injection, there is at least some connection between the crime and the punishment and, once the execution is played out, the impression is left that justice has been served. It is not just another "operation."

Delaware successfully conducted its scheduled hanging, the governor of Illinois commuted the death sentence of the woman scheduled to die there, and, ironically, the final autopsy report ruled Taylor's death at the hands of the Utah firing squad a homicide.

NOTES

1. Psychiatrist's report, in Utah State Prison files (hereafter USPF).
2. Ibid.
3. Prison memo, 17 Nov. 1976, in USPF.
4. In USPF.
5. Letter, in USPF.
6. My notes at the board of pardons hearing, 13 Aug. 1987.
7. Letter from mother of Michelle Ainsley, in USPF.
8. Board Statement, 21 Aug. 1987, in USPF.
9. Interview, 31 July 1987.
10. Letter, 24 June 1984.
11. Death Watch Log, in USPF.
12. Letter, 10 May 1988.
13. Copy in my possession, 15 Nov. 1988.

7.

DEATH ROW, COMMUTATIONS, AND PARDONS

I became the fifth man on death row one afternoon in 1984. My four cell mates on C section of maximum security were Pierre Dale Selby, William Andrews, Elroy Tilman, and Heber Norton. Arthur Gary Bishop had been sentenced to die but was being kept in a separate cell. I occupied the cell that would have been his.

A few months earlier, with the permission of prison officials, I had begun interviewing the men on death row to try to understand what the death row experience was like. How could a person live in seclusion for extended periods of time, knowing that every day brought death closer.

During my interviews the men constantly reiterated two things: the importance of routine and small things to temper the monotony of such an existence and the frustration of being totally dependant on the prison staff. Repairing a leaky toilet, trying to make a telephone call, or having a message relayed often took days, sometimes weeks. This lead to impatience, bitterness, and the suspicion that they were being purposely toyed with. They told me to spend one weekend with them, and I could multiply these feelings hundreds or thousands of times.

Now I was there. My cell (the inmates call it their "house") was ten feet long, six feet wide, and ten feet high with a metal bed and a small metal desk bolted to the floor and a toilet with a rusty, stained, and chipped seat. Everything was painted battleship blue-gray. The floor was cement, and the bars were made of solid iron. When I entered the cell, I was given a small radio so I could contact the control center, and they could contact me, in case of an emergency. If there was trouble, I was to crawl under the desk at the back of the cell and stay there. The door was locked and I was left alone.

All five cells were located in a row, each facing the same direction. A small passageway separated the cells from a cinderblock wall, the only view. Meals could be served and guards could pass by during their regular counts. To complete counts, guards were required to see some flesh of each inmate to verify that he was in the cell. There were eleven counts every twenty-four hours on death row.

Heber Norton was in the cell next to mine. He was in his mid-seventies. This made him the oldest man in the prison. He had just returned from the hospital for what was thought to have been a stroke. He was on death row for killing two female bank tellers during a robbery in Price, Utah.

Next to Norton was Pierre Dale Selby. He and William Andrews, who was two cells away from Selby at the far end of the row, were sentenced to die for killing three people at the Ogden Hi-Fi Shop. Between Selby and Andrews was Elroy Tilman's cell. Tilman was on death row for killing his girlfriend's ex-boyfriend with an axe and attempting to burn the body by setting the mattress and house on fire.

I had interviewed each of these inmates several times during the weeks prior to my own incarceration. They seemed willing to help me understand what death row was like. Andrews and Tilman were the most responsive. Selby was willing to talk but was sometimes moody, quiet, and restrained.

Norton belonged to an earlier era, when "con bosses" were respected, everyone did their own time, and nobody talked to the "screws." He did not like the way things were currently run at maximum security and he did not like blacks.

Tilman was knowledgeable about current events—national, state, and local. We talked about politics, religion, and other issues that were on his mind. He had thought things through carefully and had formed his own opinions, though they did not mirror mine.

Andrews was tierman and received a small wage for serving meals to each cell, cleaning up, and keeping things in order. Throughout my interviews I found him to be the most personable and helpful. We carried on a correspondence over several years, and he took the time to respond to questions about death row from my students. I was constantly amazed at how he was able to maintain a good attitude after his many years on death row.

As I read through the notes I took that afternoon, the feelings and smells are still very tangible:

3:38 p.m. They have just locked me on death row. I can hear the other men talking—they are teasing me. They think I ought to at least stay all night.

3:53 p.m. I've been here 15 minutes. It's too hot and my cell is dark. I can't see to read—if I had anything to read. Somewhere one of the inmates is humming, but I can't recognize the tune.

3:56 p.m. What do they do for hours—days—months—years? Nothing to see. All I can see is the white cinderblock wall across from me. There are 283 cinderblocks in my view. The only colors I can see are white and turquoise blue. Nothing else to see through my 16 bars—I counted them, too. Andrews just brought me a note from Selby and a Fortune newspaper from Tilman. Selby's note said, "I think I got burned out last Saturday or Sunday. Just don't feel like doing nothing. Just looking at the wall. That's the first time it ever happened to me. I think I just burned out."

Heber Norton was asleep when they locked me up. He now wakes up and asks Andrews who he is talking to. Andrews tells him it is Dr. Gillespie and asks him if he remembers me. Norton thinks Andrews is putting him on and swears at him. "All I want out of you is to bring me my food and stay the fuck away from me. You're no good and I'm going to show it." He next turns his anger towards the guards who apparently searched his cell after he was taken to the hospital. "I can't even find what I'm supposed to have. I don't know what they think they're accomplishing. I come back weak and upset and they fuck with my things . . . I haven't had two hours sleep in all the time I've been gone. They've had me strapped down, going everywhere in shackles—even wearing shackles to bed."

The sounds around me are muted—yet they echo. I hear pages being turned somewhere near. Quiet laughter and conversation. I hear voices of the guards coming closer. "Coming closed." Heber Norton, next door, swears, "Coming closed, that's all we hear.

Coming closed; Coming open."

4:17 p.m. They are bringing dinner. I can hear the doors clanging. One of the officers comes by to look at me. He smiles and asks if I am going to eat. I say, "Sure, got enough?" He smiles again and walks away.

4:19 p.m. The meal is served on a plastic tray: wheat roll, sliced carrots (15-18), two halves of pears, square of white cake with frosting, fried potatoes and a piece of fish. Milk and Sprite to drink. Andrews brings me my drink and passes it in through the bars. (The guards told me this would happen and that I should stand back when he brings my drink—I guess so he won't grab me?)

Meal time seems to be a time for conversation among the men on death row. They share the obligatory complaints about the meals. I ask Heber Norton how he is feeling since his return from the hospital. He replies, "Better enough to get out of the hospital, but I still feel kind of washed up." The others continue to complain about the food. They enter my conversation with Norton and ask him what he had to eat in the hospital. I am surprised by the wistfulness in his voice as he tells them, "You're not going to believe it. They give you a menu. You get to choose. I've been in a lot of hospitals. They put me in the same room as another guy. I'm eating what he's eating and everything and he's paying $450 a day. It's just like room service. I was never treated better in my life than in that hospital—even though they knew I was an inmate."

I return to my meal. Cake is too dry, potatoes are too peppery, pears are too hard.

4:45 p.m. Andrews is gathering up the trays. Conversation is subsiding. Rays from the setting sun are coming through somewhere. I can see the reflection on my 283 cinderblocks—kind of orange and dim, yet it seems brighter now than it did when I came in. If an inmate had no watch or calendar, this would be one way of marking time—the seasons, the weather, the passing of a day—all reflected on a cinderblock wall. I imagine such small things must come to have great significance over the years.
Norton is asking the others if they have been out in the "yard" during the past few days. They tell him no, and he describes how he could look out over the city from his hospital bed. "It really looked pretty at nighttime—the lights red and yellow. I just laid there in my bed looking out the window."

4:50 p.m. Norton is complaining he can't find something. Andrews tells him the guards probably took it when they searched his cell. Andrews and Norton seem to be on better terms now. I'm told feuds don't last very long on death row. They have to get along. They only have each other.

5:02 p.m. I've been on death row for an hour and 14 minutes. It's not as hard on me as I expected it would be, but it's only been 74 minutes. Seventy-four hours would be over three days, and seventy-four months would be over six years. Selby and Andrews have served more than one month for every

	minute I have been here.
5:06 p.m.	I'm getting bored and restless. Selby says he just got burned out after more than eight years and I burn out after 78 minutes? I see a place on the top of the bars where some previous occupant has marked time by putting a toothpaste dot for each day—35 days.
5:11 p.m.	I hear the guards coming for me. I don't think I would like to spend any more time than this on death row. I wonder how the others must feel as they see me walk past them on my way out and they are going nowhere?
5:38 p.m.	I just left maximum security. Now I can take a deep breath.

I remember walking outside the prison after this experience. The air was cool and a slight breeze was blowing. Storm clouds were forming over the Oquirrh Mountains, whose peaks were still snow-capped. Rush hour traffic was headed south along the freeway, and as I cleared the last security fence, I heard a rooster pheasant crowing in the field next to the prison. I was glad to be going home.

Death row today is not like it was when I left it that day in 1984. A new maximum security unit was built in 1987, and those inmates under death sentences are mixed in among the other maximum security inmates—although all are kept separate. Tilman is still there. Selby was executed in 1987; Bishop in 1988; and Andrews in 1992. Norton's death sentence was overturned, and he was given a life sentence and moved into the main population where he died on 1 March 1989 at the age of 81.

It is difficult to tell which of the remaining inmates under death sentences will actually be executed. Some sentences may be overturned, the appeals process can affect execution dates, some men may die of natural causes, and there is always the possibility of clemency. Clemency is a procedure built into the justice system that is intended to temper the politics and regional hysteria sometimes affecting high-profile crimes. Clemency takes two forms—pardons and commutations. Pardons completely abrogate legal punishment, and commutation substitutes a lesser sentence for a greater one.

In earlier times, clemencies were granted by the state or church as a gesture of grace during holidays and these became known as "holiday" or "yuletime" clemencies. For example, Jewish people anciently had the custom of granting pardons during Passover. There were also "divine intervention" clemencies. When earthquakes, storms, floods, or other natural disasters interrupted executions in process, such events were taken as signs of deity's displeasure with the proceedings and the condemned was released. There were also western American "broken rope" clemencies; the condemned was released if the rope broke during a hanging. In Germany, during the Middle Ages, the condemned could obtain release if his wife or girlfriend ran around the prison three times in the nude. In some countries whenever the coffers were depleted, pardons were sold as a means of raising revenue.

In the United States during the twentieth century pardons were also available for purchase or through political favor. In Oklahoma Governor John C. Walton pardoned 693 prisoners in eleven months, some even before the judge had pronounced sentence. Governor George W. Donaghey of Arkansas pardoned 361 convicts in one day. Governor James Ferguson of Texas granted 1,774 pardons between 1915 and 1917. Governor Miriam Ferguson, also of Texas, granted 3,500 pardons between 1925 and 1926. Some governors granted pardons or commutations because of their own opposition to the death penalty, others acted out of defiance before leaving office. Governor Lee Cruce of Oklahoma opposed capital punishment and commuted twenty-two death sentences from 1911 to 1915. Prior to leaving office in 1986, Governor Toney Anaya of New Mexico commuted the death sentences of the five men on death row. In a prepared statement he wrote: "As I have stated repeatedly, my personal beliefs do not allow me to permit the execution of an individual in the name of the State." To be sure that those on death row would not be executed by his successor, Anaya chose to commute their sentences.

In Utah no formal record has been kept of pardons and commutations. Originally this power was vested in a board consisting of the governor as chair, the state supreme court justices as members, and the attorney general of the state as secretary. In 1951 the composition of this board was changed, and the board of corrections appointed a five-member, part-time board, which sat in panels of three members. In 1983 the board of pardons was changed to a three-member, full-time board and in 1990 to a five-member, full-time board. The board of pardons has the final say about whether a condemned inmate is executed or granted a commutation.

One of the earliest stories involving the commutation of a death sentence in Utah occurred in 1857. A young soldier named Warren Drake was discovered having sexual intercourse with his horse. He was tried by court martial and sentenced along with the horse to die by firing squad. Lorenzo Brown, who was present, recorded in his journal: "He [Drake] was called out and the congregation were called upon to approve or disapprove the sentence of the court and all there in favor of the sentence were requested to uncover their heads and raise their right hand to High Heaven in token of their assent. Every head was made bare and every hand raised."[1] Brown later wrote that Drake's sentence was commuted; he was excommunicated from the Mormon church and asked to leave the territory. In the case of the mare, however, there was no commutation. The sentence was carried out and the mare was shot.

As far as I have been able to document, Utah has granted fourteen commutations of sentences for those sentenced to death. Pardons have been far fewer. I have been able to document only four pardons, although some pardons were eventually granted after a sentence had been commuted[2]

H. H. Pearson (pardoned in 1886) killed his friend during a drunken brawl while working on a cattle ranch in Utah County. Pearson was tried and found guilty of voluntary manslaughter. Shortly after the trial he was pardoned.

Jack McCormick (pardoned in 1892) was also known as Jack Emerson. McCormick was codefendant of Fred Hopt, who was executed in 1887. McCormick was pardoned by Governor Eli H. Murray after serving five years. It was the governor's last official act in office.

Ed Johnstone, acting special agent for the Castle Valley Coal Company and deputy sheriff for Emery County, was found guilty of voluntary manslaughter in the shooting death of Brigham Taylor. The jury was out twenty-four hours and returned its verdict with a recommendation for mercy. Johnstone spent about six months in prison. He was pardoned by Governor William Spry on 25 September 1913 and later became his bodyguard.

Nathan "Nick" Haworth (commuted on 21 November 1903) was sentenced to death three times. He was convicted of the murder of Thomas Sandall in Davis County. Attorneys for Haworth claimed the jurors had been prejudiced because they saw Haworth attempt an escape during his trial and a dozen or more deputies rearrest him in the courtroom in Farmington. Apparently the witnesses waiting in the courtroom to testify on Haworth's behalf were also arrested and thus a "stigma" was placed on their testimony. The board of pardons commuted his death sentence to life in prison after reviewing this trial and finding the trial had been unfair and the jury prejudiced.

The sentence of John Douglas (commuted on 22 November 1903) was commuted from life in prison to twenty-five years in recognition of his help during a prison break. He apparently obtained access to the levers that controlled the cell doors and closed them to prevent a large number of inmates from escaping.

James Lynch (commuted on 2 January 1904) and his codefendant Robert King were sentenced to death for killing Colonel Godfrey Prowse on 11 September 1900 during the holdup of the Sheep Ranch Gambling House in Salt Lake City. In the subsequent trial both were found guilty and sentenced to die. King maintained his innocence and was later released on the basis of another man's confession. Lynch was given three separate execution dates but was finally commuted to life in prison. He was granted the commutation because he saved the life of a prison guard during an escape. Testifying before the board he refused to give his real name in order to protect his parents' reputations. The board took its action believing that "a life for a life" was grounds enough to spare his life.

Charles "Dutch Charley" Botha (commuted on 5 June 1904) was convicted of murdering his fifteen-year-old wife and her lover, a respected neighbor, and was sentenced to death. During the hearing before the board, it was argued Botha had no other motive in his crime than to "protect his home and his wife's chastity." Since he killed his wife first, it was argued that the shots were fired randomly—otherwise the man would have been killed first. According to experts at the hearing, "It has never occurred in human history that a man under such circumstances would kill his wife first and then kill the destroyer of his home" (*Salt Lake Tribune,* 5 June 1904). It was also argued the trial was unfair and that the verdict could only have been "voluntary manslaughter." The board agreed and commuted his sentence to life in prison. In reporting the commutation, the *Salt Lake Tribune* stated on 5 June 1904,

> No leaden bullets will plough their way into the heart of Charles Botha next Friday morning. The five men in whose power it lay to extinguish the mysterious spark of life and turn the pulsing body into senseless clay said "live"! The death watch was removed and the dark shadow of death was dispelled. "Dutch" Charlie has entered upon that ceaseless round of rising, working, eating and sleeping within the four walls of the penitentiary which must continue until his life ends or the pardoning board exercises further clemency in this case.

Fred George (pardoned on 19 June 1904) was an accomplice to Patrick Coughlin, who was executed in 1896. George was given a life sentence because of his youth. He was paroled on 20 December 1902 and later given a full pardon "because of the exemplary life he had led."

Robert Zaffy (commuted on 19 February 1913) was originally sentenced to die for his part in the robbery of two men, one of whom was killed. He and two partners were arrested and tried. One partner was given a life sentence for his cooperation and testimony against the other two. Zaffy and Frank Romeo were sentenced to die. Zaffy's sentence was commuted to life in prison the day before his scheduled execution. Romeo was executed as scheduled.

John Cerar (commuted on 25 August 1922) was sentenced to die for the axe murder of his friend Leo Masser shortly after Cerar's arrival from Austria. The killing followed a quarrel brought on by gambling. The *Sun*, published in Price, Utah, reported on 25 August 1922: "The Board of Pardons . . . took into consideration the man's good record and the absence of any apparent motive for the murder of the friend and 'pal' of seventeen years. It was in the evidence that Cerar had been angered by losses at cards, and was probably under the influence of liquor at the time."

Noel E. White (commuted on 20 May 1934) was co-defendant in the homicide that resulted in the execution of his partner, Ralph W. Seyboldt. White was sentenced to twenty years. He served five years, eight months, five days, and his sentence was commuted by the board to time served.

Gilbert Brighton (commuted on 4 June 1934) was convicted of first degree murder. The board commuted his sentence to time served. He had served eleven years, eleven months, and nineteen days.

George Hays (commuted on 4 October 1939) was originally sentenced to death on 6 March 1939 for murdering Sherman W. Cadwell of Rush Valley, Utah. His co-defendants, William LaVern Russell, age eighteen, was given a life sentence, and Victor Montano was sentenced to ten years to life. Hays, a deaf miner, had his sentence commuted to life because of psychiatric testimony before the board that he was insane. When notified by the warden of his commutation, Hays reportedly said, "Goody! Goody!" On 13 May 1959 Hays, age eighty-five, was again heard by the board and granted a termination of sentence. He had served twenty years.

John Markham (commuted on 22 September 1941) was originally sentenced to die for killing J. G. Smith, a seventy-three-year-old magazine stand operator, during a $20 robbery. Smith was apparently hit over the head with an iron pipe. Markham was a twenty-six-year-old "bootblack" at the time of his crime. He was granted a commutation of sentence after two of Smith's children expressed no opposition as long as it meant Markham would never be free from prison. On 28 January 1960 the board of pardons granted Markham a release from prison after he had served twenty years.

Vae Monroe Fenley (commuted on 6 March 1942), at age seventeen, was sentenced to die for the robbery and murder of Royal L. Hunt, a rancher who had befriended him. The board commuted his death sentence, finding him mentally deficient. On 22 February 1959 Fenley was paroled. He was thirty-four years old at the time and had served seventeen years in prison.

Gustav Gallo (commuted in 1944) was convicted on 22 June 1928 of killing a cobbler over a $6 rent-due argument. He was ruled insane by the state supreme court on 7 February 1929 and committed to the state hospital. After five years, he was judged sane and returned to prison. The board later commuted his death sentence to life in prison, and on 6 May 1953 after serving twenty-five years, he was granted a termination of sentence and deported to his native country of Nicaragua.

Hyrum Bebee (commuted on 18 November 1948) was convicted of murdering Marshal Lon T. Larsen of Mount Pleasant, Utah, on 15 October 1945. He was sentenced to die by firing squad. His sentence was commuted to life in prison by the board of pardons. He died on 2 June 1955 at the age of eighty-five in the prison hospital of "illness incident to age." He was thought to be seventy-three years old at the time. Some still claim he was the Sundance Kid.

Fred Matteri (commuted on 11 June 1951) was sentenced to die for killing Salt Lake chiropodist Levi P. Delk. The jury had recommended life, the judge ordered the death sentence, but the board sided with the jury.[3]

Paul Buddy St. Clair (commuted on 7 January 1957) was sentenced to die for murdering Mrs. Besta Wittke of Tooele County. He was commuted after the board of pardons believed psychiatric testimony that he had a concussion at the time of the murder which led to "lack of control of emotions."

Jesse Garcia (commuted on 13 September 1962) and his codefendant, Mack Rivenburg, were sentenced to die for killing another inmate at the Utah State Prison. Garcia's sentence was commuted after Rivenburg committed suicide the day before his scheduled execution. Garcia was later paroled but has since committed additional crimes and is presently serving extended time in prison.

To have power over life and death is an awesome responsibility. On 1 July 1983 I became one of three members appointed by Utah governor Scott Matheson to the first full-time board of pardons.

Some men and women can sit day after day reading the tragedies of victim and offender and not be affected, but I could not. I had been carrying in my head for months the documentation of human tragedy: sex offenders whose lives were ruined at early ages by parents, uncles, or neighbors molesting them over an extended period; products of illegitimacy, divorce, abandonment, foster homes, death of parents, desertion, and physical abuse; addicts of alcohol, drugs, gas, glue, and other substances; families with parents, children, and relatives in prison, often doing time together; victims of incest, suicide, and tragic accidents of parents, uncles, brothers, sisters, and children.

One of my first assignments on the board was to review existing procedures for commutation hearings and to recommend new policies for the anticipated commutation hearing of Hi-Fi killers Selby and Andrews. It was several years before the hearings occurred, and when it did I was no longer on the board. But we felt at the time we would soon be called on to act in that capacity.

At this time we entered into serious discussion about our role in determining whether another human being should live or die. The two other members of that first full-time board—Gary Webster and Vickie Palacious—did eventually participate in the commutation hearing for Pierre Dale Selby. I was present too but only to document and study the process. My seat on the other side of the television cameras was much more comfortable.

Under present policy, a condemned inmate must request a commutation hearing before the board of pardons within ten days after receiving his execution date and "having completed all court proceedings." Once such a request has been received, the board sets a date for the hearing. I have been present at two commutation hearings—one for Selby and one for Andrews. Neither Gary Gilmore, Arthur Bishop, nor John Albert Taylor requested commutation, although Gilmore was given a hearing by the board after his execution had been temporarily stayed.

During such a hearing the condemned and his attorneys explain why a commutation should be granted and the state argues why the execution should proceed. The condemned usually makes a statement on his own behalf and then family or others testify as requested. The state reviews the nature of the crime and presents testimony by victims and others involved in the crime. The hearing is then closed, and the board sets a date to announce its decision. At the appointed time the board returns to the board room in the prison where the condemned inmate, attorneys, and the press have gathered, and reads its decision.

Both hearings I attended were extremely emotional. During Selby's hearing he broke down while describing his childhood. I talked with him later, and he expressed embarrassment at this show of emotion. He felt people would interpret it as a cheap attempt to save himself. During this same hearing Orin Walker, one of the victims, became emotional as he described the impact of his son's death (also one the victims) on his wife. Another victim, Courtney Naisbitt, whose mother was killed in the Hi-Fi Shop, was visibly upset during the hearing and had to leave the room.

On 21 August 1987, the board handed down its ruling that Selby had not given a compelling reason for setting aside the original sentence. At the commutation hearing for Andrews, the board's final vote was 2-1 against commutation, but less than three days prior to his scheduled execution, the Tenth Circuit Court issued a 160-day stay of execution, which was extended. As already indicated, eventually his appeals and the clock ran out.

NOTES

1. Lorenzo Brown, Diary, 1 Dec. 1857, in *Diary of Lorenzo Brown*, ed. Ben Brown (n.p.: Heritage Press, n.d.).

2. C. L. "Gunplay" Maxwell (commuted on 22 November 1903, later pardoned) was originally sentenced to eighteen years for bank robbery and murder. He served seven years and then had his sentence commuted for helping prison officials during an escape attempt. He was eventually pardoned by the governor and later became the governor's bodyguard. Fred Engelke, Robert Price, Charles Layfield, and Arnold Young all had their sentences commuted on 23 May 1904 and were eventually pardoned for aiding an escape attempt. Joseph G. Trujillo (commuted 25 August 1951) was commuted after serving approximately ten years in prison. He was paroled to New Mexico on 12 September 1963.

3. This was the last meeting of the board of pardons consisting of the governor as chair, lieutenant governor as secretary to the board, and the supreme court justices as members. After this, the board of corrections appointed a new board consisting of part-time members.

8.

OTHER EXECUTIONS AND PUNISHMENTS

Not all killers are sentenced to die. Sex, age, plea bargaining—many factors affect the outcome. Utah crimes just as bizarre and sensational as those described in this book have not resulted in executions. Also there have been a number of famous criminals with Utah connections who were imprisoned or executed elsewhere.

For example, Milda Hopkins Ashdown, age thirty-five, confessed to the 1955 killing of her forty-four-year-old husband Raymond, to whom she gave a drink of lemonade mixed with strychnine. The Ashdowns lived in Cedar City and had seven children. Mrs. Ashdown was taken into custody immediately after her husband's funeral. At the time of her arrest, her sister Elizabeth Lottie Lacey was serving a sentence in Idaho State Prison for killing her husband, Vivian Ashdown. Both sisters had married brothers. Vivian died after eating hamburgers containing strychnine.

Milda Ashdown was charged with first degree murder. A jury of eight men and four women found her guilty but recommended a sentence of life in prison rather than the death penalty. Fifth district judge Will L. Hoyt sentenced her to Utah State Prison, but at the time female prisoners served their time at the women's prison in Canon City, Colorado. Ashdown served there until 4 November 1970, when she was released.

Jean Sinclair, age forty-five, a nursing home operator, was arrested in 1963 and charged with first degree murder for the ambush killing of thirty-one-year-old Don LeRoy Foster of Salt Lake City. He was killed by a shotgun blast in the parking lot at the Susan Kay Arms Apartments, 650 North 200 West. LaRae Peterson, age thirty-two, who was in Foster's car at the time, was the object of Sinclair's affection but had recently engaged Foster. The prosecutor claimed Sinclair became jealous and after unsuccessfully attempting to hire an ex-con to do the killing she did it herself. The all-male jury found her guilty but recommended leniency. She was sentenced to life in prison and served until 15 May 1973, when she was paroled to a nursing home where she died 3 July 1973.

Iva Lee Gillian, age forty-nine, was arrested in Salt Lake City in 1967 for murdering Jesse A. Melton, age fifty-five. He was found dead in his apartment, shot in the head, and Gillian was charged with first degree murder. An all-male jury found her guilty but recommended leniency. Third district judge Marcellus K. Snow sentenced her to life in prison. She entered prison on 16 February 1968, but after an appeal overturned her conviction, she was released on 13 February 1970. She was retried and on 2 March 1970 sentenced for voluntary manslaughter.

Frances Bernice Schreuder, age forty-five, was convicted of first degree murder in 1983 for planning the killing of her seventy-six-year-old father, Franklin James Bradshaw. Her son Marc, seventeen years old at the time, did the actual killing. Testifying at his mother's trial, he said she planned the murder "so she could inherit a great deal of money very quickly" (*Salt Lake Tribune,* 20 Sept. 1983). She was convicted of first degree murder by a seven-woman, five-man jury and, although eligible for the death penalty, was sentenced to life in prison by third district judge Earnest F. Baldwin. The Utah board of pardons granted her a parole date of 8 October 1996. Her son Marc, who was certified as an adult to stand trial, was paroled in July 1994.

Other women in Utah have been involved in murders. The 5 June 1922 *Salt Lake Tribune* indicated only one woman up to that time had served time in Utah State Prison for first degree murder: Mary Jane Smith, sentenced for killing a man in 1903 with "knockout drops." She was sentenced to serve twenty years and died in prison before her sentence was completed.

The same article also identified other women who killed:

Amy Ellen Hill shot and killed Ross M. Bonney, a Salt Lake attorney who refused to marry her, in 1916. She was charged with first degree murder but later pleaded guilty to involuntary manslaughter and served her sentence of nine months in the Salt Lake county jail.

Rora Hodge in 1902 was charged in the murder of a "spectacles vendor" she was traveling with. The murder occurred on Cottonwood Creek. She apparently killed him for his money. Prior to her trial she was taken to the hospital suffering from appendicitis and committed suicide there.

Marie Arthur in 1914 shot and killed "Broadway" Jones, her lover, because he was unfaithful. The *Tribune* reported she served "several months in the County jail." After being paroled, she was subsequently charged with assault with a deadly weapon for shooting a male companion who insisted on accompanying her home from a party.

In 1922 Judge Ephraim Hansen dismissed the jury after they became deadlocked following fourteen hours of deliberation. Seventeen-year-old Angeline Wacaster was being tried for the first degree murder of Charles A. Faus, a Salt Lake businessman. Two others involved in the killing, both males, were found guilty during their first trial. Roy E.

Donnell, seventeen, who did the actual killing, was sentenced to life in prison, as was Gilbert L. Brighton, age twenty-one. Wacaster was a maid in the Faus home and plotted with the men to commit the crime. The jury deadlocked over the severity of a life sentence for such a young girl and over concerns that the board of pardons could not act in a first degree murder sentence until the person had served fifteen years. After her second trial, Wacaster was sentenced to prison and served approximately seven and a half years before being paroled.

Further evidence of Utah juries' reluctance to mete out harsh sentences to women is the case of Mrs. Leland Sneddon of Richfield, who in 1943 fatally shot her husband during a family argument in the presence of witnesses. Her husband, accompanied by another woman, had recently been arrested in an automobile theft. Sneddon admitted to involuntary manslaughter and was given a ninety-day suspended jail sentence so she could be at home to take care of her nine-month-old daughter and five-year-old son.

Some states have sentenced juveniles as young as ten and eleven years of age to death, but Utah has not, although violent crimes have been committed by juveniles. For example, George Metropolis and Dale Johnson, both escapees from Salt Lake Detention Home, were arrested after the shooting death of a night watchman in 1960. Metropolis, age fifteen, and Johnson, age fourteen, had been discovered by Gordon William Bloxham, age eighteen, who was substituting for the regular night watchman at Allied Development Company in Salt Lake City. Both juveniles were tried together as adults. They were found guilty of first degree murder, but an all-male jury recommended mercy. They were sentenced to life in prison and subsequently transferred to California. In 1970 both were freed on a writ of habeas corpus ordered by Chief Judge Willis W. Ritter, U.S. District Court for Utah. He ruled they were entitled to separate trials and that their confessions prejudiced the jury

(*Salt Lake Tribune,* 19 Sept. 1970).

Michael Patrick Jones, age sixteen, on 16 October 1963 shot and killed Detective Sergeant Marshall N. White of the Ogden police department. Jones and a companion had escaped from the Utah State Industrial School and were hiding in a nearby home when police officers began searching for them. Jones fired a shot from a rifle and hit White in the abdomen. White died a few days later. Jones pleaded guilty to first degree murder and was sentenced to life in prison. In 1968 the Marshall N. White Center, a community center for youth in Ogden, was dedicated as a memorial to White.

Brian Russell Johnson, a seventeen-year-old from Bountiful, Utah, was involved in the murder of police detective Percy L. Clark in 1973. He was tried as an adult and sentenced to serve ten years to life at the Utah State Prison. Kevin Mann Tutrow, eighteen, had the charges dropped against him when he agreed to testify against Johnson. Michael Mahoney, twenty, who apparently did the actual killing, had been killed when police returned fire.

Mark Chandler Austin, age eighteen, pleaded guilty to second degree murder in the stabbing deaths of his sixteen-year-old wife and newborn son in 1975. He received a sentence of five years to life at the Utah State Prison. His attorney blamed the crimes on "adult magazines and television" (*Salt Lake Tribune,* 17 May 1975).

Lawrence LeRoy Alexander, a fifteen-year-old from Kingston, New York, was charged in Parowan in 1976 with first degree murder and allowed to plead guilty to manslaughter in the shooting and strangling death of a thirty-seven-year-old hitchhiker. Alexander was certified as an adult and confessed to two other murders, an assault, and several robberies in a cross-country crime spree. These crimes occurred while he was an escapee from the New York Industrial School. His sentence was one to fifteen years in Utah State Prison.

Daryl Austin Babcock, seventeen years old, was certified

as an adult and tried for murder, attempted murder, and sexual assault involving two teenage Ogden girls in 1977. He pleaded guilty to first degree murder and attempted criminal homicide. Babcock killed eighteen-year-old Vicky Ann Newman by stabbing her forty-three times. The fifteen-year-old survivor of the incident was stabbed twenty times but was able to testify against Babcock. He was sentenced to life plus five years to life at Utah State Prison.

Johnny Perez, fifteen years old, was certified to stand trial as an adult in the stabbing death of Henry Topping, Jr., a sixty-five-year-old night clerk at the Ben Lomond Hotel in Ogden in 1976. Topping had been stabbed forty-four times and $370 was missing from the till. Perez was sentenced to life in prison.

John P. Miller, Jr., a fifteen-year-old Clinton boy, was arrested in 1980 and charged with first degree murder, kidnapping, and forcible sexual abuse. He had participated in the search for two-year-old Ann Hoskins, his neighbor, who had been missing for over twelve hours. When found, she had been strangled and hit over the head. There was also evidence that she had been sexually abused. Miller was certified as an adult and pleaded guilty to first degree murder and forcible sexual abuse. The Davis County attorney's office in return for the guilty plea agreed not to ask for the death penalty. Miller was sentenced to life in prison and a five-year concurrent sentence for the sexual abuse charge.

Larry Scott Webb, sixteen, and John Michael Calhoun, eighteen, killed two prominent citizens of Salt Lake City. On 27 February 1980, O. Thayne Acord and his wife Lorraine were found dead in their ransacked home. Both had been tied up and shot once in the head. Acord was part owner of the Golden Eagles hockey club, owner of Granger Builders Supply, and chair of the board of directors for Utah Bancorporation. The murders occurred while Calhoun was an escapee from the Utah State Industrial School. Both Webb and Calhoun were certified as adults to stand trial. As a result of Webb's willingness to testify about the murders, the murder charges were dropped against him and he was prosecuted only for aggravated burglary and aggravated robbery. Calhoun was found guilty of both murders and sentenced to life in prison.

In 1980 in Price, a nine-year-old boy was charged with second degree murder after he shot and killed thirty-four-year-old Cheryl Woodland. The boy went to a Mormon chapel with a neighbor after the shooting. He talked with his bishop and then returned to the scene, where he led police to a .357 magnum revolver. He was eventually committed to Utah State Hospital for treatment.

In addition to these women and juveniles, others have murdered and not been sentenced to death.

On a lonely stretch of I-80 between Coalville, Utah, and Evanston, Wyoming, Emery Dean Beck left highway patrolman William Antoniewicz, who was found by a passing motorist lying next to his patrol car, bleeding from gunshot wounds. Antoniewicz died later that night, 8 December 1974. Beck was officially charged 30 June 1976, while serving time in Wyoming State Prison on narcotics offenses. He was apparently transporting drugs at the time Antoniewicz stopped him. Earlier in the day Beck had broken into the Lyman, Wyoming, jail, taking drugs held there in evidence and aiding the escape of Wayne Tague, a friend who was incarcerated. Beck left Tague in Salt Lake City and was returning to Wyoming when he was pulled over. He shot Antoniewicz as he approached Beck's car. Charged with first degree murder, Beck's first trial resulted in a hung jury. Prior to his second trial, he pleaded guilty to second degree murder and was sentenced to five years to life—this sentence to run concurrent with his sentence in Wyoming. Beck was eventually paroled in 1989.

In April 1978 police were led to a stand of Junipers outside of Kanab, where the bodies of two missing French tourists were discovered tied to the trees. The bodies had been in the same location for over a year without being discovered. Wayne Richard Brewer, age twenty-two, and Rodger Kipp Andreason, age nineteen, were both charged with first-degree murder. Both men originally pleaded innocent and then later changed their plea to guilty of second-degree murder. Both claimed to have been on drugs at the time of the killing and indicated they had been hitchhiking when they were picked up by the two tourists. While sitting in the back seat of the rented car, they conceived the plan to rob and kill the tourists and then steal the car. The car was later driven to Salt Lake City and turned in at the airport. Brewer and Andreason were sentenced to five years to life and given an added six-year term for using a firearm. Brewer was paroled in 1990 and Andreason a few years later.

On 20 August 1980 Joseph Paul Franklin (who legally changed his original name of James Clayton Vaughn, Jr.) shot and killed two young black joggers as they crossed 500 East at 900 South near Liberty Park in Salt Lake City. They were jogging with two white female teenagers, neither of whom was killed although one girl was grazed by a passing bullet. Franklin was arrested in Lakeland, Florida, after escaping from a Kentucky police station where his car had been impounded and he was being questioned about a stolen car. Returned to Utah, he was tried on federal charges of "violating the civil rights of the two black youths." He was found guilty by a ten-female, two-male jury and sentenced to two consecutive life terms in prison. Between the time the verdict was handed down and the sentence imposed, Franklin was suspected of many other killings with racial overtones, including double homicides in Oklahoma, Indiana, Ohio, and Pennsylvania. Franklin was also later tried in the shooting of Vernon Jordan, Urban League director, in Fort Wayne, Indiana, and the bombing attack that crippled Larry Flynt, publisher of *Hustler* magazine. He is presently incarcerated at the federal maximum security prison in Marion, Illinois.

Michael P. Moore, a twenty-five-year-old University of Utah engineering student, was arrested, charged, and found guilty of the 5 March 1982 double killing of Jordan Rasmussen and Buddy R. Booth. Moore was the manager of Log Haven Restaurant in Mill Creek Canyon near Salt Lake. Fearing that Rasmussen, a restaurant bookkeeper, was part of an organized crime ring attempting to take over the restaurant, Moore shot and killed him. Booth, a laundry truck driver, arrived on the scene shortly after the killing of Rasmussen. Booth was killed to keep him from talking after he discovered Rasmussen's body. Originally charged with two counts of capital homicide, at his trial Moore admitted the killings but argued he should have been charged with manslaughter not capital homicide. He was found guilty of the two counts of capital homicide, but after deliberating for one hour during the penalty phase, the jury brought back two life sentences to run consecutively. Moore is still at Utah State Prison.

Ervil LeBaron, referred to as a polygamist cult leader, was arrested for the 11 May 1977 murder of Rulon Allred. The actual killing was done by two women, but LeBaron was charged as the mastermind behind the killing. Allred's death apparently resulted from a power struggle among competing polygamous sects. LeBaron allegedly ordered the killing of Allred so he could take over Allred's group. A jury of nine men and three women found LeBaron guilty of first degree murder and conspiracy to commit murder. He was sentenced to serve two life sentences but died at Utah State Prison on 16 August 1981—apparently of a heart attack. He was fifty-six years old.

Rena Lei Chynoweth, believed to be one of the women who did the actual killing, was acquitted after her trial on charges similar to those faced by LeBaron. In 1990 she published her own version of the affair and admitted she had in fact killed Allred. Because Chynoweth was acquitted of murder charges, she cannot be recharged with the murder.

On 24 July 1984 Ron and Dan Lafferty drove to the home of their youngest brother Allen, where they killed his wife Brenda and baby daughter Erica by cutting their throats. The two Lafferty brothers claimed to have followed a revelation from God: "Thus saith the Lord unto my servents [sic] the prophets. It is my will and commandment that ye remove the following individuals in order that my work might go forward. For they have truly become obstacles in my path and I will not allow my work to be stopped. First thy brother's wife Brenda and her baby, then Chloe Low, and then Richard Stowe." Both Laffertys were arrested 7 August 1984 at Circus Circus in Las Vegas, Nevada. In a separate trial, Dan Lafferty was convicted of the two murders, but because the jury was unable to reach a unanimous decision for the death penalty, he was given two life sentences. Two members of the jury claimed Dan Lafferty had manipulated them by "psycho-sexual seduction."

Ron Lafferty was not as fortunate. His trial was postponed after an unsuccessful attempt to hang himself, and on 7 May he was found guilty and sentenced to die. Later his death sentence was overturned. He was brought to trial a second time, found guilty, and again sentenced to die. He awaits execution for the two murders, while Dan serves his time with the main population at Utah State Prison.

On 15 October 1985 Steven Christensen was killed in his office by a home-made bomb. A few miles away Kathleen Sheets picked up a small package in the walkway of her home and was killed by a bomb blast. On 16 October 1985 Mark Hofmann was injured by a bomb blast shortly after getting into his car at 200 North Main Street. Evidence at the scene of this last blast tied Hofmann to the other two deaths as well as to an intrigue that involved document forgeries. In a plea bargain prior to trial, Hofmann pleaded guilty to two counts of second-degree murder and two counts of communication fraud. In exchange twenty-six felony counts were dismissed, and Hofmann was sentenced to five years to life for killing

Cartoon lampooning the sentencing of Mark Hoffman. Appeared in the *Ogden Standard-Examiner*, 12 August 1987. By permission of Calvin Grondahl.

Christensen and also given three separate prison terms of one to fifteen years for the murder of Sheets and for theft convictions. The board of pardons gave Hofmann a sentence of "natural life," implying they intend no parole for him.

On 18 January 1979 John Singer was surrounded by law enforcement officers as he picked up his mail. A few minutes later he lay dead on the snow, ending a two-year conflict that began with Singer's decision to keep his children out of public schools. His wife Vickie and their six children were left alone. On 16 January 1988 a Mormon stake center in Marion, Utah, was bombed, and police followed three sets of footprints crossing a snow-covered field to the home of Vickie Singer, where she and fourteen other people had barricaded themselves. This standoff eventually involved more than one hundred and fifty law enforcement officials and ended with the death of one of them, ccorrections officer Fred House.

John Timothy Singer, who it was believed fired the fatal shot, was charged with murder. Addam Swapp, who had married two of John Singer's daughters, and Vickie Singer were charged with assault and explosives violations. The motive for the bombing was apparently related to the expectation that John Singer would be resurrected and return to his family near the anniversary of his death. After a trial on federal charges, Addam Swapp was found guilty and sentenced to fifteen years in prison for the bombing and for exchanging shots with federal agents. Vickie Singer was given a five-year sentence for her role in the shootout, and Timothy Singer, her son, and Jonathan Swapp, her son-in-law's brother, each received ten-year sentences for firearm charges along with five years probation on other charges. Addam Swapp and John Timothy Singer were later convicted of reduced homicide charges in state courts, and Jonathan Swapp was convicted of negligent homicide. Vickie Singer was released from prison in June 1991. The others are still serving their sentences.

Many of Utah's famous criminals have committed

crimes in other states. Alfred Packer was one of twenty men who left Salt Lake City in 1873 for the gold fields of Colorado and became snowbound in the Colorado Rockies. It is believed that Packer killed five companions and lived by eating their flesh until he wandered into the Indian Agency in February 1874. He claimed the group, because of hunger, began attacking each other and eating the loser. Packer evaded arrest and was not seen again until 1883 when a member of the original group of twenty recognized him in Salt Lake City. He was arrested and returned to Lake City, Colorado, where he was tried, convicted, and sentenced to die. Later on appeal he was granted a new trial, charged with manslaughter, and sentenced to forty years in prison. He served sixteen of these, was released in 1901, and died in 1907.

Butch Cassidy and his "hole-in-the-wall" gang also had Utah connections. Many of them came from Utah, and their escapades brought them into the state frequently—sometimes for extended periods of time.

On 5 June 1981 Jack Abbot was released from Utah State Prison. His book, *In the Belly of the Beast,* which he wrote in prison, had just been published with the encouragement and assistance of Norman Mailer. After his release, he obtained an out-of-state parole to a federal half-way house in New York. While basking in the popularity of his book, he went to a bar and, after an argument, he and Richard Adan, a twenty-two-year-old waiter, stepped outside. A short while later Adan was found dead on the sidewalk. Abbot was arrested in the Louisiana oil fields two months later. He was charged with murder and at his trial found guilty of first degree manslaughter. Abbot was sentenced to fifteen years to life and will begin serving the sentence after he finishes the remaining eight years of the original sentence for which he was on parole from Utah.

One of the most widely publicized "Utahns" executed in another state was Ted Bundy, a University of Utah law student from Washington. Originally Bundy was arrested in Salt Lake City for possession of burglary tools. He had been stopped for speeding, but in the car officers found among other things: "an ice pick, a pair of handcuffs, silk stockings with holes cut in for eyes and nose, and other items a burglar might carry" (Stephen G. Michaud and Hugh Aynesworth, *The Only Living Witness* [New York: Signet Books, 1983], 87).

On 2 October 1975 after being identified in a lineup, Bundy was charged with kidnapping and attempted murder. He went to trial on 23 February 1976 for an attempt to kidnap and assault Carol DeRonch at Fashion Place Mall in Murray. He waived a jury trial, was found guilty, and sentenced to a term of one to fifteen years in Utah State Prison. A few months later on 27 January 1977, Bundy was extradited to Colorado to stand trial for the murder of Caryn Campbell. During his first appearance in court in Colorado, he jumped out of a courthouse window during a recess and escaped. Recaptured the following 13 June, he escaped again on 30 December and was not captured again until Florida police found him on 14 February 1978—after the Chi Omega sorority murders and the sexual assault and murder of twelve-year-old Kimberly Diane Leach. Bundy was found guilty and sentenced to death for these murders. He was executed in Florida's electric chair in January 1989. Prior to his execution he met with law enforcement officials to clear up other unsolved killings. He granted a filmed interview in which he blamed pornography for his problem. Anywhere from thirty to fifty killings of young girls across the United States have been attributed to Bundy. In one of his last telephone conversations with his mother in Tacoma, he said, "I'm sorry I've given you such grief . . . but a part of me was hidden, all the time" (*Ogden Standard Examiner,* 24 Jan. 1989). He has been the subject of five books and a television miniseries entitled *The Deliberate Stranger.*

Presently one young Utahn is awaiting execution in Nevada. Edward Bennett and Joseph Beeson, both from central Utah, were arrested, tried, and found guilty of the "thrill kill" of Michelle Moore, who was shot to death during the robbery of a convenience store near the Las Vegas Strip. Beeson avoided the death penalty by agreeing to testify against Bennett. Bennett was sentenced to be executed. Beeson was given two life terms without possibility of parole. On 20 August 1990 Beeson was found dead in his cell, strangled and stabbed to death with a home-made weapon resembling an ice pick.

It is difficult to predict the future direction of executions in Utah. Other Utahns will undoubtedly be involved in capital crimes in Utah and in other states, and their executions will, of course, depend on a variety of factors. It is doubtful that Utah will begin executing convicts under the age of 18. Nor is it likely that the state will begin executing women or even sentencing them to death for capital offenses.

There seems to be little question that Utah will continue to impose the death sentence. Public opinion polls have consistently shown high levels of support among the populace. Despite this, there have only been thirty-eight executions since statehood in 1896 and only eleven during the forty years previous to that.

EPILOGUE

In 1987 the old cemetery at the Utah State Prison was excavated. The graves of inmates who had died in prison had been moved twice before—once from the Sugarhouse prison to Point of the Mountain and again from there to make way for Interstate 15. Unmarked and untended, the graves were moved a third time to a permanent place in the Salt Lake City cemetery.

We will probably never know exactly how many inmates were buried in prison, nor all their names. We do know, however, that among them are Fred Hopt, Enoch Davis, Frank Rose, Jules Szirmay, Nick Oblizalo, and Edward McGowan.

We also know that Joe Hill is not among them. After his cremation most of his ashes were scattered. One envelope found its way to the National Archives and was eventually given to the Industrial Workers of the World (IWW) in 1988. In 1991, the ghost of Joe Hill revived briefly as the IWW commemorated the 75th anniversary of his death.

Unremembered and unforgiven, the majority of Utah's

executed men lie in obscurity. Perhaps it is better this way. Heartache and sorrow accompanied the crimes and deaths of these men and their victims.

I have stood outside the houses where their unfathomable crimes took place—quiet residential areas, bustling business districts, and lonely stretches of highway. Many of the buildings no longer stand, others are dilapidated, while some still have people living in them—people who are oblivious to the terrible tragedies that occurred in their bedrooms, kitchens, and living rooms.

I have stood on the sagebrush flats of Sage Hollow where Patrick Coughlin was executed by firing squad; in windy Mountain Meadows where John D. Lee died sitting on his coffin; and on the bench above Tooele where Robert Sutton was executed and buried. I have interviewed those who were present at executions, including one who as a young boy was taken by his father to stand outside the prison walls while Joe Hill died inside. I have stood beside the gurney on three separate occassions as men were quickly and quietly strapped down to die.

I have climbed to the old culvert where the body of John Stallings was discovered after Eliseo Mares dumped it in the ditch near Hoytsville; visited the grave of Constable Stagg who died at Palmer's cabin; and paid my respects at the graves of other victims. I have visited with the families and friends of victims and come to feel the sense of tragedy and sorrow that accompanies such losses.

I have found many of the graves of the men who paid for these losses. Several are buried near family and loved ones—including some who were their victims. Many others lie totally forgotten.

In my mind are many nagging, unanswered questions about the place of capital punishment in society. Questions about the why's and how's of crime; about trials, guilt, and sentences; about what it means.

I have no doubt that we will continue to sanction capital

punishment. There should, however, be a method whereby we learn something from their deaths.

The answers, like the questions, are complex. Yet in some fundamental way they may be as simple as this poem (which hangs on my wall) written in 1979 by David Allen Osborne while on Idaho's death row:

How I came to be here
God please let others see
Let them have a chance to change
Before someday they are me
For how I came to be here
Is a story both long and short
Because of many mistakes I've made
I was sent here by the court
Just how I came to be here
Is contained in some report
Of how I've wagered and how I've lost
And broken some rules for sport
Yes how I came to be here
It's all been written down
So let them see what becomes
Of a man who plays the clown
Yes it is written there for all to see
So let them read it all
Before they end up just like me
Behind some prison wall
But how I came to be here
Should be quite simple to tell
One does not get to Heaven
When he walks the Road to Hell!